Anchorage
A Pictorial History

Anchorage

A Pictorial History

by Claus-M. Naske and
L. J. Rowinski

Design by Jamie Backus Raynor

Donning
Virginia Beach/Norfolk

SECOND STAGE OF WORK IN ANC

RAGE NEW 12 FT. CONCRETE WALKS.

The Donning Company/Publishers
5659 Virginia Beach Boulevard
Norfolk, Virginia 23502

Library of Congress Cataloging in Publication Data

Naske, Claus-M
    Anchorage, a pictorial history.

    Bibliography: p.
    Includes index.

    1. Anchorage, Alaska—Description—Views.
2. Anchorage, Alaska—History—Pictorial works.
I. Rowinski, Ludwig J., 1929–   II. Title.
F914.A5N37   979.8′3   80-28128
ISBN 0-89865-106-9 (pbk.)

Printed in the United States of America

Contents

Foreword   8

Preface 11

Introduction 12

Chapter One
    Early Inhabitants of the
    Cook Inlet Area 15

Chapter Two
    Knik: 1890-1914 29

Chapter Three
    Tent City at Ship Creek:
    1914-1915 39

Chapter Four
    The Townsite Takes Shape:
    1916-1919 55

Chapter Five
    The Incorporated Town:
    1920-1940 101

Chapter Six
    Years of Transition: 1940-1960 125

Chapter Seven
    After Statehood: 1960-1980 157

Bibliography 204

Index 205

Foreword

From its modest beginnings as the anchorage of supply barges for Alaska Engineering Commission to its position today as the population and commercial hub of the 49th state, Anchorage has demonstrated that it will continue to progress.

It hasn't always been easy. In the two and a half decades following its founding, Anchorage was populated by a hardy citizenry that could breathe somewhat easier in the short summer months, but the winters were entirely another matter. Until the beginning of World War II, when Alaska's strategic position was recognized in relation to both our allies and our adversaries, Anchorage hung on.

At the end of 1941 Anchorage was a smaller community than was Seward. We had a population of about 2,000 when I came over the mountains from Valdez to work in the start of construction of Fort Richardson, Anchorage's U. S. Army post.

After the war Anchorage's growth really began in earnest. With the dedicated efforts of many private citizens and public officials, Anchorage's population growth continued on a healthy upward climb. The conversion of military jobs to civilian positions assured the community a degree of permanence of residents that had escaped us during the war years. The build up of peacetime defense programs and electronic warning systems boosted Alaska's construction industry through the 1950s.

The Cook Inlet oil discovery gave credence to Alaskans' longstanding assertion that our natural resources were deserving of the long range look that our boom-and-bust economy had never seen.

Before Alaska's North Slope oil was discovered and the trans-Alaska oil pipeline project was receiving national and international attention, Alaska was primarily known for its winters and its earthquake. It was Good Friday of 1964 when Southcentral Alaska was rocked by an earthquake of 8.6 magnitude on the Richter scale. While the quake itself was a natural phenomenon deserving considerable attention, the reconstruction that took place immediately thereafter was another noteworthy event.

By the end of the 60s the North Slope oil discovery and the impending construction of the oil pipeline distracted the rest of the world from the other realities of Alaska and Anchorage. While the pipeline brought Anchorage and the rest of the state unprecedented prosperity, it also brought with it the problems of a small population in the midst of the largest private construction project in history.

Now, in the post-pipeline construction years we find ourselves preparing for the use of Anchorage's share of Alaska's oil wealth. There are those who want cash in hand and a return to the "good ole days" of boom and bust. There are others who would put our revenues in the bank for the proverbial rainy day.

Anchorage, by and large, wants to see its benefits dedicated to making this community a more liveable place, even though it is an exceptionally liveable city already.

We are expanding on our existing base of cultural and recreational facilities to support our growing population and our visitor industry at the same time. We're planning for the future at a rate that was always impossible in the past. Then we were lucky to achieve survival. We consider ourselves fortunate to finally be in a position to look beyond the coming winter.

We're making Anchorage liveable for all— the young, the old, the newcomer and the long-time resident. Some of the families that started Anchorage in the teens have descendants living here still. We want to insure that there is always a place for those who have made such huge contributions to our community. They deserve the opportunity to remain, rather than retire in the Lower 48.

A visitor to Anchorage today would recognize quite a few of the buildings in this volume because we've made a sincere effort to retain that piece of the past that our first buildings represent. We invite any and all interested travelers to come north and see it first hand. In our brief history we've made some remarkable progress. And its only the beginning. There's much more to come.

George M. Sullivan
Mayor, Municipality of
Anchorage

July 29, 1981

The first local airline company was Anchorage Air Transports. Art Shonbeck was president, and Russell Merrill was the first pilot. Shonbeck also owned the Ford agency in Anchorage during the 1920s. Courtesy of Anchorage Historical and Fine Arts Museum

Preface

Anchorage is a young, isolated city; but also it is a city of change and growth. Built originally as a center for construction of the Alaska Railroad in 1915, it did not incorporate until 1920. Some of the major events that affected the rest of the country such as the Depression of the 1930s, the Matanuska Colony, and World War II, as well as the 1964 earthquake and coal and oil development in Alaska also influenced the urbanization of Anchorage. The town grew into a typical American city with services and conveniences expected in modern cities. But Anchorage's uniqueness lies in its enviable spectacular setting and in its civic enthusiasm that makes every change a challenge and a promise for a better future.

We have tried to capture some of the characteristics of change, and we have used photographs to reflect many of those changes over the last sixty-five years. Of course Anchorage's inhabitants know there will be many more changes and expect their city to become bigger and still better tomorrow.

Assembling the pictures was possible only with the help of many people and organizations. Sincere thanks are due to Diane Brenner, Archivist, Anchorage Historical and Fine Arts Museum; Renee Blahuta, Library Assistant, Archives, University of Alaska, Fairbanks; Phyllis DeMuth, Librarian, Alaska Historical Library; John Cloe, Historian, Office of History, Alaska Air Command; as well as Richard Reeve, Mrs. Albert (Mary) Dyer, Mrs. Norma Hoyt, Anchorage Fur Rendezvous, Port of Anchorage, John Mattsen of the Chugach National Forest of the U.S. Forest Service, Anchorage Convention and Visitor Bureau, the University of Alaska, Anchorage, Anchorage Community College, and Alaska Pacific University.

This book contains only a sample of the photographs that are available to illustrate the history of Alaska's largest city. We realize others might have chosen differently and found additional sources. However, the hunt for photographs is fascinating, and we hope this effort will encourage the further preservation of and use of photographic materials in our state.

Introduction

Anchorage, Alaska's largest city, is located on Cook Inlet in southcentral Alaska. Sourdoughs and Cheechakos (oldtimers and greenhorns) alike cannot help but be impressed, time and again, by the grand and impressive country surrounding this area. To the north of the inlet towers the snow-capped Aleutian Range with its several extinct as well as active volcanoes. This range merges with the Alaska Range and its great peaks, including Mounts Foraker, Hunter, and McKinley. To the east of the inlet lies the Kenai Peninsula. Glaciated lowlands of ground moraine and outwash plains border the Kenai and Chugach mountain ranges with their glaciers and ice fields. Finally, beyond the upper reach of Knik Arm rise the rugged ridges of the Talkeetna Mountains, which complete the mountainous ring around the Cook Inlet basin.

The whole region is marked by a fairly moderate climate with four well-marked seasons. About half of Alaska's population lives here, ample proof that the weather is fairly benign. It is the tempering influence of the Japanese Current and the proximity of the surrounding mountains which determines the climate. The Chugach Range keeps out the warm, moist air from the Gulf of Alaska, resulting in a mere 10 to 15 percent of the precipitation common on the Gulf of Alaska side. The Alaska Range, on the other hand, stops the cold air coming from the northern interior. Winter extends from mid-October to mid-April, with periods of clear, cold weather alternating with cloudy, mild conditions. Although Cook Inlet has much floating ice, the high tidal fluctuations maintain at least some open water throughout the year. Also, snow does not normally accumulate to more than fifteen inches.

Mid-April break-up is accompanied by warm days and cold nights while the mean temperatures rise rapidly. Summer extends from June to early September. Precipitation is

Quiet shorelines and majestic mountains were seen by Captain Cook as he reached the Turnagain Arm area of Cook Inlet. This modern picture shows some of the ski runs at the Alyesksa ski resort

very slight up to mid-July, when average cloudiness increases, and the remainder of the summer is wet. Fall is brief and lasts only from early September to mid-October. Precipitation drops noticeably, and mild days are followed by chilly nights, occasionally punctuated by autumn storms from the southern Bering Sea and Bristol Bay with occasional wind gusts considerably exceeding fifty miles per hour.

Vegetation varies considerably. Timberline ranges anywhere from 1,000 to 2,500 feet, with an

at the left. The mining town of Girwood developed at the base of that mountain. Courtesy of U.S.D.A., Forest Service, Chugach National Forest

mosses, lichens, and various grasses.

The wildlife population of the Cook Inlet region is considerable. Nearly a third of Alaska's moose thrive here because of the favorable range conditions brought about by human-caused fires. Also, Dall sheep occupy the higher elevations of the Talkeetna, Chugach, and Kenai mountains as well as the Alaska Range. There are even some goats in the eastern mountains. Brown grizzly bears exist in small numbers, while black bears are relatively abundant. Most of the smaller fur-bearing animals are plentiful, too. Upland game birds are represented by three ptarmigan species as well as the spruce grouse. The coastal lowlands around Cook Inlet support limited numbers of breeding waterfowl, but during the fall migration south, thousands of ducks and geese stop here to rest.

In prehistoric times, Eskimo and Indian cultures met in the region. Later, competing Russian traders settled here, mined the first gold and coal, and also utilized the abundant salmon. Explorers from various nations conducted reconnaissance voyages, and here is where the federal government laid out Alaska's first planned city, and also established its first substantial agricultural community. The region also contains the state's major transportation hub in Anchorage, including air, water, rail, and highway connections. Anchorage International Airport serves scores of global polar flights across the top of the world each day. It also serves hundreds of domestic and intrastate flights linking Alaska's communities and cities with each other as well as with the forty-nine states. Nature favored the area with a moderate climate, fostering settlement. Here live approximately one-half of the state's population. Anchorage has become the financial and political capital of the state. In short, here is where the action is.

average of 1,500 feet. Spruce, hemlock, aspen, alder, mountain ash, and groves of cottonwood and small birch trees are found in many of the valleys. Alder and willow thickets extend to an elevation of roughly 2,000–2,500 feet. Many of the valleys are filled with tangled masses of fallen trees and underbrush, including mountain cedar, devils club, blueberries, cranberries, currants, and raspberries as well as a variety of smaller plants and many flowers throughout the summer. The alpine slopes are covered with

Chapter One

Early Inhabitants of the Cook Inlet Area

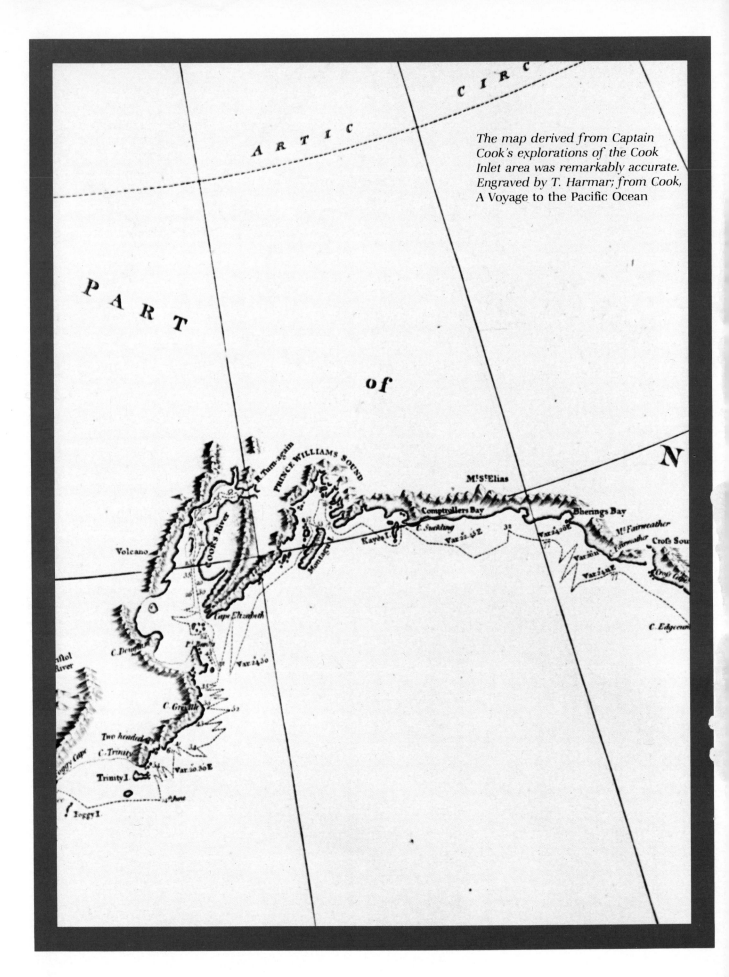

The map derived from Captain Cook's explorations of the Cook Inlet area was remarkably accurate. Engraved by T. Harmar; from Cook, A Voyage to the Pacific Ocean

It seems certain that a sparse Tanaina Indian population occupied the Cook Inlet region by the 1770s and 1780s, subsisting entirely on the fisheries and wildlife resources. These peoples were relatively late arrivals, archaeologists suspect, since Pacific Eskimos occupied the Cook Inlet region, at least seasonally, beginning sometime before A.D. 1000 and lasting after A.D. 1000, perhaps as late as A.D. 1700. The Tanaina Indians apparently moved into the area no earlier than A.D. 1650 and no later than the 1770s, when a number of Europeans encountered them, including Captains James Cook, Nathaniel Portlock, George Dixon, and John Meares.

It was, however, Captain James Cook, England's most famous navigator, who reconnoitered the northwest coast of North America on his third and last voyage. On May 21, 1778, he sighted off the southeastern coast of the Kenai

Portrait of Captain Cook from Voyages Round the World performed by Captain James Cook F. R. S., 1822. *Courtesy of Archives, University of Alaska, Fairbanks*

Peninsula a high promontory which he named Cape Elizabeth after the princess whose birthday was that day. Eventually, Cook saw more land bearing west-southwest. Driven off by a heavy northwest gale, he came back towards Cape Elizabeth. On May 23 he saw more land that seemed to connect the cape with the land farther to the west. The next day Cook had a closer view of another cape, the northeastern extremity of an island, which he called Saint Hermogenes Isle (Marmot Island) and Cape Saint Hermogenes. Beyond lay the snow covered mountains.

Between the two capes there was a fifty to sixty mile gap of open water. Cook decided to investigate the wide opening, the entrance to Cook Inlet. At daybreak on May 26, Saint Augustine's Day, Cook sighted what seemed to be a chain of islands to the northwest. The nearest of these, a cone-shaped mountain of great height, he called Mount Saint Augustine. As the haze cleared, Cook observed the summits of a mountain range, rising from low land visible everywhere. Seeing this, Cook immediately concluded that they would "find no passage." Nevertheless, to please others in the party, Cook spent until June 6 examining the inlet.

On May 30, Cook's ship, the *Resolution*, passed two headlands. John Gore, a lieutenant on the ship, named the land on the eastern shore "Nancy's Foreland," after his "Favourite Female Acquaintance;" the other he called "Gore's Head." Later cartographers simply named them East and West Foreland. When the ships had been anchored under a bluff on the eastern shore, Natives of the inlet made their first visit: two men in kayaks apparently wanted someone to land. Instead, Cook followed the shore as it turned east. Before turning back, Cook sent boats to explore Knik Arm, past the present-day location of Anchorage, and Turnagain Arm. Because of the strong tide, the boats could not enter the latter. As a departing gesture, Cook then sent Lieutenant James King to take possession of the land and the river.

The lieutenant and his party lowered a boat and rowed toward the land against the strong tides. A group of friendly Natives met them "who were happy to observe a turf turned and the flag flown, shared the bottled porter in which King George's health was drunk, and accept the empty bottles." King buried one bottle, containing papers relevant to taking possession, under some rocks by the side of a stunted tree, "where

17

if it escapes the Indians, in many ages hence it may Puzle Antiquarians."

As the ships sailed down the inlet, Indians approached the shore, "flying one of their leather frocks on a pole as a sign of peace, or standing with arms spread wide." Cook observed that the Natives had considerable amounts of iron in the form of spears and long knives, and remarked that they "made no attempt to depart with anything that they had not acquired by honest trade." Cook thought that the iron must have come from people directly in touch with Russian traders—which these people could not be; for, as Cook reasoned, if the Russians had been here, they would have taken in trade all the available sea otter skins which they prized highly. Instead, these skins still were a common article of clothing.

Cook did not name the inlet, however, and Lieutenant King merely referred to it as the "Great River." Later on, in London, Lord Sandwich ordered that it should be called "Cook's River." In 1792, George Vancouver altered the word "river" to "inlet."

Captain Cook had written in 1778 that "there is not the least doubt that a very beneficial fur trade might be carried on with the inhabitants of this vast coast. But unless a Northern passage should be found practicable, it seems rather too remote for Great Britain to receive any emolument from it." Despite Cook's remark, a British trading company sent two of his own men, Nathaniel Portlock and George Dixon, on the ships *King George* and *Queen Charlotte*, to the North Pacific a year after the publication of Cook's *Voyage*. The Englishmen found that the Russians already were in Cook Inlet. William Beresford, on board the *Queen Charlotte*, met the Russians in the summer of 1786. The British learned that the Russians had come from Unalaska in a sloop and had brought along with them Kodiak Natives "the better to facilitate their traffice with the inhabitants of Cook's River, and the adjacent country." Beresford noted, however, that the Russians were on extremely poor terms with the Native inhabitants of the region.

Nevertheless, in 1786 the Russian Shelekhov-Golikov Company established a post called Alexandrovsk at English Bay near the mouth of Cook Inlet. Also, in 1787 a rival company, Lebedev-Lastochkin, founded Fort Saint George at Kasilof, farther up the inlet, then in 1791 also established Nikolaevsk Redoubt at Kenai, above

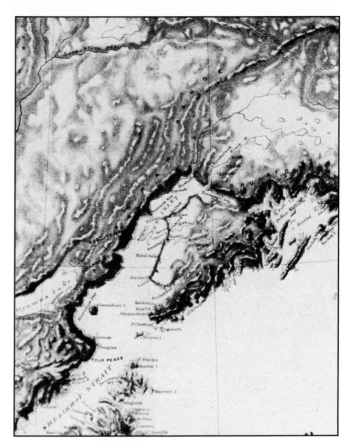

Ivan Petroff, a special agent for the Tenth United States Census in 1880, compiled a map of Alaska and the adjoining regions. This portion shows the Cook Inlet area.

Kasilof. Despite their foothold along the inlet, the Russians felt harassed by the English and Spanish competition for the fur trade.

Foreign competition in the Cook Inlet area, however, proved to be minor and temporary. Much more serious was the fierce struggle for the trade between rival Russian firms, the Lebedev-Lastochkin and Shelekhov-Golikov firms along the inlet, a competition finally ended when Tsar Paul I granted a monopoly to the Shelekhov-Golikov group. The new organization, the Russian-American Company, quickly came to grips with many problems under the dynamic leadership of its manager, Alexander Baranov.

By 1850, former Russian employees had established small agricultural settlements along the Cook Inlet at Seldovia, Ninilchik, and Eklutna. In 1849 the Russian-American Company sent Petr Doroshin, a mining engineer, to search for minerals along Cook Inlet. For two seasons, Doroshin investigated the several valleys, streams, and canyons of the Kenai River area. He found small amounts of gold in almost

Portage Pass once was a major access route from Prince William Sound to Cook Inlet. It has been used since prehistoric times by the native people of the area and was a popular winter route to the Kenai and Cook Inlet areas during the mining days in the late 1800s and early 1900s. Changes in Portage Glacier have made this route difficult today. Parts of the trail were still visible in 1963. Courtesy of U.S.D.A., Forest Service, Chugach National Forest

all of these locations, and his report on coal deposits at Port Graham resulted in the opening of a mine there.

In 1867, the Russians, who faced pressing diplomatic problems in Asia and Europe and for whom the North American colony had simply become a logistical problem, sold Alaska to the United States for the sum of $7,200,000. The United States Army quickly took over the territory in Sitka, in October 1867, and supervised the transfer from Russian to American control. Not until 1869 did troops arrive to construct and occupy Fort Kenai. There, however, was little need for the Army because the Natives were quiescent, and by the fall of 1870 the garrison had left Fort Kenai.

The fur trade continued as an important economic activity, and in 1868 three small trading posts were established at Knik, Kenai, and English Bay. Although the pelt of the sea otter was by far the most valuable commodity in the fur trade along Alaska's Pacific coast west of Cape Saint Elias between 1867 and 1900, a variety of other fur-bearing animals, such as mink, marten, land otter, several varieties of foxes, beaver, muskrat, bear, lynx, and wolverine were important as well. Several natural trade routes funneled the furs of the backcountry toward Cook Inlet. Indians as far away as the headwaters of the Copper River used the valley of the Matanuska River to deal with trading schooners in Cook Inlet. They later dealt at Knik Station after it had been established. The Susitna River and its various tributaries carried hunters and trappers to Tyonek, where a station was built at an early date, and later at Susitna Station on the Susitna River. Trappers used the Kenai River and its lake system to carry the furs from much of the peninsula toward the station at its mouth. There also were a number of small trade routes on the western side of the inlet, the most important of which probably was the portage from Iliamna Lake.

The Alaska Commercial Company had started building trading stations on Cook Inlet in 1868, and by the end of the century it owned and

operated a dozen of these, extending from Cape Douglas in the south to the head of Knik Arm in the north. And although the Alaska Commercial Company was by far the biggest organization, a handful of smaller trading companies offered competition along Cook Inlet and also built several shore stations. By the turn of the century, however, the fur trade had declined so sharply that most stations closed.

In the twentieth century, several of the settlements along Cook Inlet grew in population, and the general merchandise stores which dealt with furs merely as a sideline supplanted the traditional trading posts. With improvements in the transportation system, itinerant fur buyers made their rounds, and soon many fur producers shipped their wares directly to fur houses in Seattle, San Francisco, St. Louis, and New York.

Fishing and fish processing were major activities on Cook Inlet after the turn of the century and had been important for at least twenty years before that. Over the years, operators built dozens of fish-packing plants on the shores of the inlet and on the banks of the various rivers flowing into it. Thousands of fishing vessels harvested the bounty of the inlet waters from the Barren Island to Knik Arm. And while the salmon fishery provided the greatest financial returns, herring, halibut, crabs, and clams also contributed to the economy of the Cook Inlet region.

A Native family near Kasilof on the western shore of the Kenai Peninsula. The man is identified as Humpy. The Russians had already established themselves in the area in the late 1700s. Later a cannery was built and some beach mining was carried on. About 1890. Courtesy of Wetherbee Collection, Archives, University of Alaska, Fairbanks

Natives of the upper Inlet about 1890. Courtesy of Wetherbee Collection, Archives, University of Alaska, Fairbanks

Natives caches, or storage buildings, near Cook Inlet about 1890. Salmon are drying on the rack at the right and a light sled is on the ground. Courtesy of Wetherbee Collection, Archives, University of Alaska, Fairbanks

Evan Jackaloff, "one of the old time Russians," and his family. The photo was probably taken near Kasilof about 1890. To the left is a rack with salmon drying. Courtesy of Wetherbee Collection, Archives, University of Alaska, Fairbanks

The bark Corea *out of San Francisco ran aground about 1890 on Kalgin Island Reef with twelve feet of water in her hold. Fish from the canneries would probably have been her principle cargo. Courtesy of Wetherbee Collection, Archives, University of Alaska, Fairbanks*

H. M. Wetherbee of San Francisco made four voyages to the Cook Inlet area between 1889 and 1892. He was a competent photographer and labeled this photo of himself "The Artist." The mooseskin shirt he is wearing was a traditional garment among the Indians of the area. It is decorated with Dentalium shells as are his caribou skin boots. The snowshoes would appear to serve no purpose at this season. A large brown bear lies behind him. Courtesy of Wetherbee Collection, Archives, University of Alaska, Fairbanks

The unnamed companion of H. M. Wetherbee is comfortable in their "sitting room" in Kasilof. A practical device is the water heater on the stove. Probably unusual for Alaska about 1890 are the spats on the gentleman. Courtesy of Wetherbee Collection, Archives, University of Alaska, Fairbanks

The Arctic Fishing Company Cannery at Kasilof about 1890. Courtesy of Wetherbee Collection, Archives, University of Alaska, Fairbanks

"All hands building traps, May 1890." Fish traps were built out into tidal areas in many parts of Alaska to catch salmon for the large cannery operations. Courtesy of Wetherbee Collection, Archives, University of Alaska, Fairbanks

The crew of the Aberdeen Cannery on Cook Inlet in 1890. Courtesy of Wetherbee Collection, Archives, University of Alaska, Fairbanks

The Kenai Cannery, 1890. Note the tracks running out on the dock. Courtesy of Wetherbee Collection, Archives, University of Alaska, Fairbanks

This neatly built log cabin on the west side of Cook Inlet at Tyonic was called "fisherman's camp" by Wetherbee. It appears to be shut up tightly with a small notice on the door. Courtesy of Wetherbee Collection, Archives, University of Alaska, Fairbanks

Snug Harbor, in Cook Inlet, apparently had a late snow on June 1, 1890. The figure in the long coat appears to be H. M. Wetherbee. Courtesy of Wetherbee Collection, Archives, University of Alaska, Fairbanks

The steep Crow Pass Trail led from Girwood to the Eagle River area, across Knik Arm from Knik, and was part of the famous Iditarod Trail. Courtesy of U.S.D.A., Forest Service, Chugach National Forest

Chapter Two

Knik:

1890-1914

The Town of Sunrise was founded in 1895 by a group of goldseekers including John L. "Jerry" Odale, who named the town and built a two-story house there. Soon there were over 100 claims filed on Sixmile Creek and other creeks in the area. By 1944 the town was essentially deserted and today no buildings remain. Courtesy of National Archives Collection, Archives, University of Alaska, Fairbanks

By the late 1800s, the region contained a number of traders and settlers. In 1886 residents of the area organized the Cleveland Mining District, and thereafter numerous entrepreneurs engaged in small coal mining ventures in the region, mostly on the northern shore of Kachemak Bay. The North Pacific Mining and Transportation Company, the Alaska Coal Company, and the Cook Inlet Coal Fields Company probably conducted the most extensive coal mining operations.

Around 1880, one George W. Palmer kept a store at Knik Arm, another branch of Cook Inlet, and by the 1890s, prospectors found gold on Resurrection Creek, a stream emptying into Turnagain Arm. Soon there were a trading post at Sunrise on Turnagain Arm and a small mining camp at Hope on Ressurrection Creek. Miners rushed twice to the area, once in 1896 and again in 1898. But the Sunrise district was not a great goldfield: from 1895 to 1900 it produced $780,000; from 1901 to 1906 the output totaled only $543,000, supporting approximately 200 miners. Despite the small population, Sunrise had three trading posts in 1897–1898, and this meant slim pickings for all; by 1900, there were two, and in 1901 only one was left. Like the gold, the population continued to dwindle so that by 1910 the last trading post had closed its doors.

In the meantime, miners and prospectors had laboriously hacked out primitive trails connecting the scattered camps and ultimately unifying the region between Cook Inlet on the south and the Talkeetna Mountains on the north, the Matanuska River in the east and the Susitna River in the west. The old trading post at Knik served as a supply center for the Willow Creek Mining District, organized in 1898. Residents received their supplies from small vessels which landed at Knik. As hard rock followed placer mining, the population grew to several hundred, and Knik became a small but viable community. Yet placer mining turned out to be a relatively unimportant activity because the combined efforts of various operators produced only approximately $30,000 in the Willow Creek Mining District between 1897 and 1914. This was not enough economic activity to nourish hopes and ambitions for a town of Knik.

Fortunately, however, a number of things happened elsewhere in Alaska to positively affect the town in the early years of the twentieth century. Among these was the start of construction of the Alaska Central Railroad, extending northward from the new town of Seward on Resurrection Bay. In the Tanana Valley, in the interior of Alaska, Felix Pedro made a gold strike near a site which soon grew into the town of Fairbanks. These and other discoveries led to more intensive prospecting everywhere, and soon gold lode finds were made in the Talkeetna Mountains to the north of Knik and placer gold was found on the Iditarod River far to the northwest. Knik quickly became the major trading center for the gold and coal mines for the greater region, and it also supplied the various sawmills in the Matanuska Valley, the Susitna River Basin, and the Willow Creek Mining

The Coast Range Mining Company had a mill at the edge of the tidelands near the mouth of Bear Creek near the town of Hope. Hope was the center for the mining activity on Bear and Resurrection Creeks. Hope remained as a fading mining town until the 1964 earthquake, when land subsidence damaged many of the old buildings. The community still has some permanent residents and some summer homes. Courtesy of National Archives Collection, Archives, University of Alaska, Fairbanks

District. Although the population never exceeded 500, the new discoveries helped the town economically.

Although the summer traffic to the Iditarod proceeded by way of the Yukon and its tributaries, in winter the shortest route between the Iditarod discoveries and an open port was overland to Seward. Because it happened to be squarely on the trail, the little settlement of Knik soon also became the major stopping point along the route. In addition, the Seward Chamber of Commerce dispatched two men to locate and publicize the winter route. As an added sign of Knik's importance, the federal government established a post office in 1905. By 1910 Knik had a population of 118, while the Matanuska Valley contained approximately 500 settlers. There were also several trading posts as well as other businesses.

The mining in the Willow Creek District during the summer months and travel over the Iditarod Trail in the winter promoted the growth of Knik. Residents would long remember January 10, 1912, when two freight sleds pulled by thirty-three dogs loaded with 2,600 pounds of gold arrived at the town from Iditarod on the Kuskokwim River.

By 1914 the town had acquired its own four-page weekly, the *Knik News*. It could also boast of two trading posts, three roadhouses and hotels, a restaurant, a general hardware store, a saloon, a transfer and fuel company, a school, and J. T. Harvey's building and construction business.

The Palace of Sweets sold candies, tobacco, magazines, stationery, and postcards. Two dentists and two physicians ministered to the health needs of the community, and itinerant priests of the Russian Orthodox Church occasionally looked after the spiritual requirements of their flock. From 1911 until 1914, W. H. O'Connor represented the law as the marshal of Knik.

Cabbage, kale, and turnips grown by Herman Stetler near Hope are displayed with pride. The produce rests on a simple sled in front of a home made of unpeeled logs. Courtesy of National Archives Collection, Archives, University of Alaska, Fairbanks

Small ships, both sail and steam, plyed the waters of Cook Inlet in the late 1800s and early 1900s serving the canneries, mining communities, and trading settlements. Courtesy of Anchorage Historical and Fine Arts Museum

Since one summer and one winter route radiated from Knik into the mining district, an all-season road had to be constructed in order to handle the heavy machinery needed for lode mining operations. Three operators apparently got together and built such a wagon road. The Bartholf brothers fashioned the lower portion, which included a bridge across the Little Susitna River. Robert Hatcher continued the road up to what is now known as Hatcher Creek and over Hatcher Pass. It is unclear what part the Carle outfit had in building the road, but early maps designated the twenty-six mile route as the "Carle Wagon Road," so it can be assumed that the designation was earned.

In short, Knik prospered for several years and remained the transportation and distribution center for much of the upper Cook Inlet region. However, the Alaska Railroad Act of 1914—which led to the development of Anchorage—resulted in the eventual abandonment of the once-thriving community of Knik.

While Anchorage grew, the settlement of Knik declined. In May 1916 the town lost its post office, and, although it was reopened in 1917, it closed for good that same year. The railroad reached the head of the Knik Arm and then pushed across the lower part of the valley toward the Susitna. Soon Wasilla, a new settlement on the line, developed. Not only did the new town enjoy rail transportation, but Wasilla also was much closer than Knik to both the homesteaders and the miners in the region. Therefore, Knik continued to decline. Businesses moved to Wasilla or to Anchorage, and the residences either were abandoned or were moved to new locations—until Knik had become a ghost town.

KNIK ALASKA LAKE STREET

Knik was a small trading center for the miners and settlers in the area as well as an important stop on the Iditarod Trail. Lake Street ran through a group of neat log buildings that must have been a haven of civilization for people at remote mines and on traplines. *Courtesy of Herning Collection, Archives, University of Alaska, Fairbanks*

Knik was never a very large community but it had a developing waterfront, roadhouses for those moving through by dogsled or ship, and some small farms that tried to provide some of the community's needs. *Courtesy of Anchorage Historical and Fine Arts Museum*

This group in front of the Pioneer Roadhouse in Knik in the early 1900s is unidentified except for Leopold David, who was the U.S. Commissioner there from 1910 until his move to Anchorage in 1915. He continued to serve as Commissioner until 1921. He is the fifth man from the left in the front row, wearing a rather formal suit and a tie. Courtesy of Anchorage Historical and Fine Arts Museum

The Knik Trading Company, circa 1900. Courtesy of Herning Collection, Archives, University of Alaska, Fairbanks

Mrs. Leopold David and her daughter, Caroline, posed outside their Knik home in 1914. Courtesy of Anchorage Historical and Fine Arts Museum

A view of the interior of the David home in Knik about 1914 shows possessions that would have been prized in an isolated Alaskan community. Everything in the photo would have been shipped in from "Outside." Courtesy of Anchorage Historical and Fine Arts Museum

An ad from the Cook Inlet Pioneer for G. W. Palmer's store in Knik. Ship arrivals were looked forward to since many necessities of life in pioneer communities were sent by sea from Seattle and other west coast ports. Courtesy of Anchorage Historical and Fine Arts Museum

In 1914 Portage Glacier was already part of the Chugach National Forest, but the face of the glacier was closer to the present parking lot than it is now. This view is from the west shore of the lake looking up Bear Creek. Jack Brown, a forest ranger, and his wife Nellie came to live at Ship Creek in 1912. Courtesy of U.S.D.A., Forest Service, Chugach National Forest

Two families lived in the Ship Creek area before the railroad development began. The J. D. Whitneys and the Jim St. Sinclairs were joined in 1912 by Jack and Nellie Brown. Jack Brown came as one of the first rangers to the Chugach National Forest. A cabin was located in the trees on the right in this photo which is supposed to have been taken in 1912. Courtesy of Anchorage Historical and Fine Arts Museum

Tyonic in 1906 was an Indian village and a trading post. This group includes Fitzsimmons, Nayley, Shumacher, David, Furgeson, Hussey, Burkhardt, Tyler, Cureny, Davis, Furgeson, Captain Shaw, Martin, and Purser Zymic. Unfortunately the names are not keyed to the numbers on the photo. Perhaps the presence of the two ship's officers indicates an imminent departure. Courtesy of Anchorage Historical and Fine Arts Museum

Chapter Three

Tent City
at
Ship Creek:

1914-1915

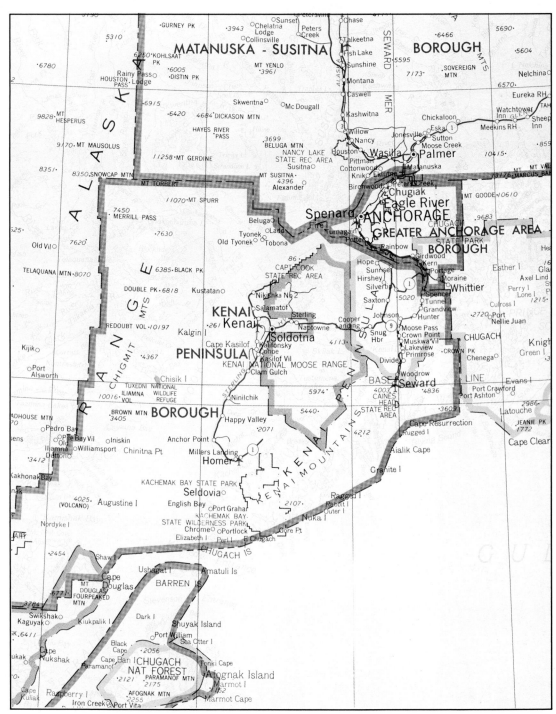

UNITED STATES
DEPARTMENT OF THE INTERIOR
GEOLOGICAL SURVEY

A L A S K A

MAP B

COMPILED FROM THE GEOLOGICAL SURVEY ALASKA TOPOGRAPHIC MAPS
SCALE 1:250 000, AND OTHER OFFICIAL SOURCES
MODIFIED TRANSVERSE MERCATOR PROJECTION

SCALE 1:1 584 000
1 INCH EQUALS 25 MILES

50   50   100   150 MILES

50   0   50   100   150 KILOMETRES

CONTOUR INTERVAL 1000 FEET
NATIONAL GEODETIC VERTICAL DATUM OF 1929

THIS MAP IS AVAILABLE WITH OR WITHOUT CONTOURS
FOR SALE BY U.S. GEOLOGICAL SURVEY
FAIRBANKS, ALASKA 99701, DENVER, COLORADO 80225, OR RESTON, VIRGINIA 22092

Anchorage and the Cook Inlet region.

Four routes were considered possible for the Alaska Railroad. The western route from Seward to Fairbanks was chosen by President Woodrow Wilson, and Ship Creek became the base for construction of the line to the north.

The tent city, which later became the major railroad yard, still showed signs of the newly cleared forest in 1915. Courtesy of Helen Van Campen Collection, Archives, University of Alaska, Fairbanks

Prior to the summer of 1915, the area which is now Anchorage was known by various names, but primarily as Ship Creek. That name was used because the settlement expanded from the mouth of that stream. After larger boats began to navigate the upper reaches of the inlet, the waters off Ship Creek became known as Knik Anchorage. From here smaller craft could reach the town of Knik or the settlement at Ship Creek. Congress passed the Alaska Railroad Act in 1914, President Woodrow Wilson signed the measure into law that same year, and the secretary of the interior appointed an Alaska Engineering Commission, composed of geologist Thomas Riggs, Jr., and two experienced railroad builders, William C. Edes and Frederick Mears. Under the direction of this commission, eleven survey parties spent the summer of 1914 examining possible routes for the proposed railroad but did not recommend any specific one in the final report. Nevertheless, rumors about the impending construction attracted individuals to settle at Ship Creek, and soon the term Knik Anchorage was used in various published materials. On April 10, 1915, President Wilson selected the so-called western or Susitna route, running from Seward (a year-round ice-free port on tidewater) through the Kenai Peninsula, the Matanuska Valley and its coal deposits, and to the Nenana lignite coal fields. Officials not only hoped these fields might end the Fairbanks fuel famine and perhaps revive the declining placer gold mining industry but also hoped that coal from the Matanuska fields already proven in steaming tests, could be shipped from Ship Creek on Knik Arm to outside markets. Although longer than some of the other routes and presenting numerous difficult engineering problems, this choice offered the most promise for future development of the natural resources. An initial appropriation of $35 million started the project. Thus began a unique five-year experiment in federal operation of a frontier town, some 3,500 miles distant from the seat of the national government.

As early as February 1915, rumors had begun circulating that work soon would begin on constructing a line between Ship Creek on Cook Inlet and the Matanuska coal fields. This set off a rush to the creek flats, reminiscent of earlier mining stampedes—but with a difference: the federal government intended to control the area in and around the rail yards so that no private interests could impede the project, hoping to allow the town, itself, to develop in an orderly manner.

Frederick Mears, a member of the Alaska Engineering Commission, landed at the mouth of Ship Creek in late April 1915 to direct the operations at the site. He found a stampede town of approximately 2,000 souls who were living in ragged tents and temporary wooden buildings under unsanitary conditions. The first settlers established themselves on the northern shore across the creek from present downtown Anchorage. In addition, each week at least 100 more adventurers debarked from steamers or walked in from the end of the Alaska Northern Railway, which the federal government had purchased to form the first seventy miles of the railroad out of Seward.

It was the United States Post Office Department which gave the town the name Anchorage. In April 1915 preparations for establishing a Post Office were made, and Roydon Chase received the appointment as the first postmaster. All mail was to be sent to Anchorage and not Ship Creek. The Alaska Engineering Commission protested, maintaining that the name would cause confusion, but maps and news accounts quickly adopted the name Anchorage. But in August 1915, residents were afforded the opportunity to decide the name of the town by a vote. Alaska's Governor John F. Strong thought that Matanuska was the most appropriate name because linking the Matanuska coal fields by rail was the initial goal of the AEC. Numerous other names were suggested which included: Alaska City, Ship Creek, Winalaska, Gateway, Anchorage, Terminal, Homestead and Lane, the latter in honor of Secretary of the Interior Franklin K. Lane. In the end the majority of residents cast their vote for Alaska City. The federal government, however, concluded that a change would be unwarranted, and despite petitions by the Chamber of Commerce to the AEC, Anchorage it remained.

The view from Government Hill showed the tent city spread across the Ship Creek basin in July of 1915. The log building at the right in the picture was an early Alaska Engineering Commission building. Courtesy of Vide Bartlett Collection, Archives, University of Alaska, Fairbanks

Even in the temporary town, some solidly constructed buildings appeared, many of which were moved to the new townsite. The building to the right of the Kootnay Inn is the Crescent Hotel, which continued business in the new town. Courtesy of Pyatt Collection, Alaska Historical Library

"First camp of Government Railroad, Anchorage, Alaska." Helen Van Campen, visiting the site in 1915, looks into her temporary quarters. Courtesy of Helen Van Campen Collection, Archives, University of Alaska, Fairbanks

In the meantime, Mears, who was an experienced construction engineer and army officer, directed building activities at the site. Soon, however, he became frustrated over delays and various problems; in fact, by May 1915 he had also become very concerned about the commission surgeon's warning of contaminated water if the temporary settlement on the flats continued much longer. Mears, therefore, quickly urged the General Land Office to survey the high, timbered tableland south of the camp so that lot sales on the permanent site could begin as soon as possible.

Workers came to Ship Creek from every state in the Union, and there were immigrants as well, particularly Scandinavians. Many of the arrivals were restless and rootless workers who departed when the railroad was completed. However, many families did establish roots in the tent city and the townsite which became Anchorage. Oscar Anderson, for example, arrived at Ship Creek in 1915 and with a partner named Jensen developed the primary meat packing company for the region. The Ship Creek Meat Market later relocated to Fourth Avenue, and Anderson lived in Anchorage until 1974.

From the rugged existence at the tent city, the roots of a permanent Anchorage spread.

Water in the tent city came from a few wells, from "springs," or from Ship Creek. Courtesy of Anchorage Historical and Fine Arts Museum

The original caption for this photo is "Daddy's helpers; a familiar scene as the new town went up." From the beginning, whole families came to Anchorage to help build the new town. Courtesy of Anchorage Historical and Fine Arts Museum

"Waiting for the mail." The United States Post Office assigned the name of Anchorage to the new town although the Alaska Engineering Commission preferred Ship Creek. Roydon Chase was appointed the first postmaster. The building was moved to the new townsite and used until a new post office was built in 1916. Courtesy of Anchorage Historical and Fine Arts Museum

One of the businesses in the tent city, 1915. Courtesy of C. L. Andrews Collection, Alaska Historical Library

Entrepreneurs set up businesses along this street in the tent city. Many men came to the area hoping for work on the railroad construction project. Courtesy of Helen Van Campen Collection, Archives, University of Alaska, Fairbanks.

In this "street" scene in the tent city, the well-dressed woman at left carefully makes her way through the stumps and debris of the newly cleared area. Courtesy of Pyatt Photo, Alaska Historical Library

Dick and Dave's Chophouse provided information on shipping and contact with a local signpainter. Many Alaskans from other towns and camps as well as newcomers came to Ship Creek with the hope for success in a new place. Courtesy of Alaska Historical Library

Baseball games are a Fourth of July tradition everywhere in the United States. Here is Anchorage's first—July 4, 1915. Courtesy of Anchorage Historical and Fine Arts Museum

This photograph is identified as Joe Curten and the builder of the first residence on Government Hill, 1915. The structure seems to make effective use of unaltered native materials. Courtesy of Anchorage Historical and Fine Arts Museum

The first tracks in the Ship Creek basin in 1915, before the tent city had vanished. Courtesy of Alaska Historical Library

The Montana Pool Room was one of the businesses which eventually moved to the new townsite. In this view, some of the first tracks run through the camp. Courtesy of Archives, University of Alaska, Fairbanks

The old channel of Ship Creek wound through the basin below the present city. When the channel was realigned in the 1920s, the marshy areas and shoreline were filled in, but the mouth of the creek is still in its original location. The tracks led from the shore, where lighters were unloaded, to the main construction area. Smaller boats were unloaded along the bank of the creek, the area where the crowd is gathered. Courtesy of Anchorage Historical and Fine Arts Museum

Landing Passengers at Anchorage, Alaska

Because large ships could not unload directly on shore, passengers and freight had to be lightered ashore. Here, two boats are approaching their Anchorage landing. The Ship Creek area is between Government Hill on the left and the Anchorage townsite on the plateau to the right. Paddle-wheelers similar to the one in the picture were also used for freighting up the Matanuska and Susitna rivers. *Courtesy of Anchorage Historical and Fine Arts Museum*

The first government rails were laid on the short run to the shore of Cook Inlet, where barges brought in goods from ships anchored offshore. *Courtesy of Helen Van Campen Collection, Archives, University of Alaska, Fairbanks*

Ties were laid for the rails to the shoreline area, where lighters would be unloaded. *Courtesy of Anchorage Historical and Fine Arts Museum*

Two Alaska Engineering Commission lighters were drawn up on shore, May 1915. Tracks led to the main supply staging area. Courtesy of Helen Van Campen Collection, Archives, University of Alaska, Fairbanks

A part of the Alaska Engineering Commission material yard is shown in a view from Government Hill, circa 1916. Courtesy of Lulu Fairbanks Collection, Archives, University of Alaska, Fairbanks

Before the docks were built, ships had to anchor offshore. Goods were transferred to barges and lightered to shore. Here is a miscellaneous cargo including lumber, pipe, bales of hay, and many cases and crates, including one for E. A. Blewett of Knik. Courtesy of Helen Van Campen Collection, Archives, University of Alaska, Fairbanks

Driving piles for Dock Number One near the mouth of Ship Creek. Courtesy of Helen Van Campen Collection, Archives, University of Alaska, Fairbanks

Ocean Dock under construction, around 1918. Courtesy of Alaska Engineering Commission, Alaska Historical Library

The Admiral Watson at Ocean Dock on July 28, 1919. This dock, which served Anchorage until it was closed in the mid-1920s, was an improvement over Dock Number One since larger ships could be tied up here. Courtesy of Alaska Engineering Commission, Alaska Historical Library

Looking toward Government Hill across the Ship Creek basin, the Alaska Engineering Commission complex lay beyond the lumber yard (in the foreground). On the hill were Alaska Engineering Commission cottages, some of which had been completed in October 1915. Courtesy of Anchorage Historical and Fine Arts Museum

Dock facilities grew rapidly along the shore. Here, the Annie W. is landing passengers from the S.S. Mariposa, May 29, 1917. The Alaska Engineering Commission hospital is on the ridge in the background. Courtesy of Anchorage Historical and Fine Arts Museum

Chapter Four

The Townsite Takes Shape:

1916-1919

"The new townsite of Anchorage." A road was built from the Ship Creek basin to the higher ground where the townsite was located. Courtesy of Anchorage Historical and Fine Arts Museum

Early in May 1915, Andrew Christensen, the land office chief in charge of surveys, completed the survey of the 350-acre Anchorage townsite.

On June 19, President Wilson issued the "Alaska Railroad Townsite Regulations," which provided detailed rules for the conditional sale of lots at public auction. No lot was to be sold for less than $25, and the purchaser had to pay either in full or one-third down and the balance in five equal installments. One clause reflected hopes for high standards of sobriety and behavior by unruly construction workers: the lots and the payments for them would be forfeited if the property were "used for the purpose of manufacturing, selling, or otherwise disposing of intoxicating liquors as a beverage, or for gambling, prostitution, or any unlawful purpose..." If a purchaser fulfilled the conditions, he would receive a patent to the land at the end of five years.

The auction of lots took place on July 10. Christensen, acting as superintendent of sales, promised the prospective bidders permanent improvements and large federal expenditures in Anchorage. His optimistic speech spurred the pioneers into active competition for business and residential lots. After he closed the sale on July 18, 1915, Christensen reported that 655 lots had brought just under $150,000. However, the Land Office, and later the Commission, continued to sell lots and tracts and to lease business sites in the terminal area.

A removal order cleared residents from Ship Creek flats, and soon the town spread over the rectangular pattern of the Land Office survey. As engineers concerned with railroad building, Commission officials had no experience with town planning. They named east-west streets numerically and north-south streets alphabetically.

Actually, government activities had begun in April 1915 when Frederick Mears landed at Ship Creek and opened a post office. Mears and Commission Chairman William C. Edes appointed a physician to be sanitary officer and selected a special agent of the Land Office, J. A. Moore, to be temporary townsite manager. The two officials drew up and issued sanitation and fire control regulations.

On September 1, 1915, Secretary of the Interior Franklin K. Lane authorized the installation of a water system, and the Commission began pumping water from a sand filter bed in Ship Creek to the townsite above. In 1916 the Commission installed a telephone system and began construction of a power generating plant.

In September 1916 Christensen reported that a total of 1,108 lots had been sold in Anchorage, and he estimated that the city had a population of approximately 4,500. Overlapping functions and divided responsibilities necessitated conferences between Christensen, Mears, J. A. Moore, the temporary townsite manager, and J. G. Watts, the townsite engineer where policy and townsite administrative matters were decided. An accountant, a clerk who also doubled as stenographer, and a nightwatchman helped to administer the town.

The Commission was not altogether happy with the arrangement because it wanted to build

Three hundred fifty acres were cleared on the plateau south of Ship Creek. Lots, 50 feet by 140 feet, were laid out along streets set out in a grid pattern that was typical of railroad towns of the period. This photo, July 12, 1915, shows the new townsite as it appeared to bidders at the auction. Courtesy of Pyatt Collection, Alaska Historical Library

the railroad rather than administer the town. Yet townspeople preferred federal direction, assuming that a non-profit Commission could furnish cheaper utilities and various other improvements.

There was much inefficiency in the system. The Land Office, for example, was responsible for investigating and reporting all violations of townsite regulations, including failure to pay improvement assessments; the Commission, on the other hand, was expected to make improvements, to issue assessments, and to have general authority over the townsite. Overlapping functions and divided responsibilities necessitated conferences between Land Office and townsite officials. Finally, in August 1915, Christensen and the commissioners decided to create a Land and Industrial Department of the Commission to supervise most matters outside the sphere of engineering and construction. Secretary Lane signed the order creating the department on April 12, 1916, at Seward, but it later moved to Anchorage.

In spite of government efforts, bootlegging, gambling, and prostitution flourished in the new town. The licensed saloon at Knik, thirty miles from Anchorage, supplied much of the "booze." There were wide open gambling games, and characters with nicknames such as "Dago Jim," "Creampuff Bill," and "The Pale-Faced Kid" brought a certain professionalism to the games.

In shacks and tents southeast of the town, some thirty or forty prostitutes "entertained" the construction workers. The Commission and the deputy marshal's office shared responsibilities for restricting the prostitutes, who were forbidden to mingle on the main street with the townspeople, to one section of the town. Some Commission members, however, disturbed by the lax attitude of the marshal's office toward the various vices, harbored the well-founded suspicion that members of the marshal's office were profiting from bootlegging, gambling, and prostitution. Conditions improved considerably after the arrival of the permanent deputy marshal in January 1917.

In December of 1917 Christensen reported that Anchorage had a population of approximately 5,000 people, down from a summer's high of about 6,500. After completion of railroad construction in the vicinity of Anchorage in the fall, many workers left the town for the states.

By 1916 Anchorage had two schools: a day school with 7 teachers and 300 students, and a night school with 10 teachers and approximately 200 students. During the 1916–17 school year, the Commission had assumed responsibility for the maintenance and operation of the Anchorage public schools, but territorial and federal funds for this purpose had been inadequate. Since the federal government retained control of the town lots, Anchorage residents could not incorporate in order to raise revenues for school support and maintenance. Residents concluded, therefore, that because the federal government had failed to foresee the school situation, it should accept responsibility for financing education.

On March 3, 1917, Congress passed legisla-

tion empowering the territorial legislature to establish and maintain schools. Thus, School boards of unincorporated towns could incorporate school districts and could assess and collect taxes. The territory would pay 75 percent of the cost of maintaining the schools. By year's end, five school board members administered the three-story-high Anchorage school which had "sewer connections, electric light, and is modern in every respect...."

In December 1917 Anchorage boasted of 1,349 buildings, valued at approximately $1 million while total property values as fixed by the Anchorage School District assessor amounted to over $2 million. Anchorage had become a substantial community by the end of 1917. Four physicians, 6 dentists, 7 lawyers, 2 engineers, and 2 architects practiced their professions. There were shops for clothing, food, drugs, and other necessities, and there were 11 billiard halls.

Several fraternal organizations were represented, such as the Masonic Lodge, the Odd-fellows, the Elks, and the Moose Lodges. Also there were 5 churches in the community: the Roman Catholic, Christian Science, Congregational, Episcopal, and Presbyterian.

Demands grew for creation of a group similar to a city council to advise on townsite management. Soon, an Advisory Council was established whose seven members were to be elected at-large by adult lot owners, a requirement which eliminated the large transient population. Chosen in 1917, the Advisory Council, however, failed to supplant the role the Chamber had played.

Anchorage residents were directly affected by the financial demands of the townsite office. By the end of 1917, the Commission had expended some $125,000 which included construction of the water and sewer systems, street improvements and sidewalk construction, health and sanitary services, and maintenance and operation. The townsite manager and his assistants dealt with both small and large issues of management. They issued detailed regulations, including a warning to dog-team drivers to keep off the sidewalks; also, believing that they were responsible for controlling loose dogs, they operated a pound.

Commission administration contributed much to the amenities of life in Anchorage. It built a hospital for its employees, open to others as well; constructed a dock; ran excursion trains;

The auction of townsite lots on July 10, 1915, was conducted by Andrew Christensen. As chief of the Alaska field division of the General Land Office, Christensen was involved with the development of a townsite and later helped guide the growth of the community. The first lot sold for $825. Lots along Fourth Avenue brought the highest prices since it would be the main business street in the town. Courtesy of Alaska Engineering Commission, Alaska Historical Library

This photo of August 1915 shows progress along Fourth Avenue a month after the auction. New buildings are going up, some tents from the Ship Creek area have been moved into place, and businesses are operating. Courtesy of Anchorage Historical and Fine Arts Museum

1917 Businesses

Bakeries	3	Garages	2
Banks	2	Grocers	6
Barber Shops	10	Hardware	2
Bath, Turkish	2	Hotels	12
Billiard & Pool		Jewelers	4
Halls	11	Laundries, Steam	1
Blacksmiths	1	Lunch Counters	2
Brick yards	1	Meat Markets	3
Building Material	5	Men's Furnish-	
Bunk houses	9	ings	10
Cigars	1	Notions	1
Cleaners	2	Office Equipment	1
Coal Dealers	3	Photographers	3
Concrete Blocks,		Photo Supplies	1
Tile, etc.	1	Plumbers &	
Candy Makers	1	Tinsmiths	5
Confectionary,		Printing Offices	3
Stationery		Restaurants	15
& Periodicals	6	Soft Drinks	3
Dairies	2	Tailors	4
Department		Theatres	2
Stores	2	Transfer Com-	
Drug Stores	3	panies	5
Dry Goods, Ladies		Undertakers	2
Furnishings	2	Wallpaper, Paints,	
Electric Supplies	2	etc.	4
Furniture	2		

founded a YMCA; encouraged gardening, athletics, and beautification; established parks and recreational reserves; and even helped to control the spread of influenza during the 1918 epidemic. Near the end of 1917, the town reached a population peak of 3,928 permanent residents. Summer construction usually added substantial numbers; but now World War I affected the population, some moving to the States, where better employment opportunities existed.

World War I affected Anchorage and the railroad adversely. Even before the United States entered the war, the preparedness boom in 1916 drew men from the railroad. While the Alaska Engineering Commission employed a record workforce of 5,675 in 1917, a shortage of un-skilled labor and track men hampered construc-tion. In 1918 the working force averaged only 2,800, and about half of the Commission's clerical and engineering forces enlisted in the armed services. Mears resigned in January 1918, to accept a colonelcy and command of the 31st Engineer Regiment which served on the French railroad system. Many men left with the colonel. Women filled some jobs, while others went unfilled. High wages elsewhere and diminishing appropriations perpetuated the labor shortage through the 1920 season. During 1919 the Commission even hired Native laborers to fill the work force, a desperate step at that time. Southcentral, interior and northwestern Alaska all lost population during the war, and only southeastern Alaska gained population. Anchorage skidded from 3,928 in 1917 to 1,856 in 1920.

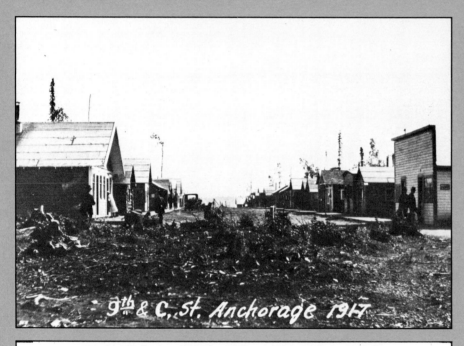

From Ninth Avenue this view down C Street looked north toward the business area. The blocks south of Ninth Avenue were originally cleared as a fire break, to separate the community from the forest beyond. The rough ground in the foreground later was used as an airfield, then became the Park Strip and subsequently became Delaney Park. Courtesy of Anchorage Historical and Fine Arts Musuem

COOK INLET PIONEER

AND KNIK NEWS

VOL. 1   Anchorage, Alaska, Saturday, June 5, 1915   NO. 1

Railroad Work Is Under Way At Anchorage

Anchorage, the coal terminal, presents a scene of activity, due to the construction of the big government railway system now getting fairly under way here. A slight delay has been incurred because of the shortage of cer-tain kinds of food supplies in the government commissary, but an early steamer will relieve this situation and things will move along more vigorously and more contracts will be awarded.

In town, the chief activity is along the water front. Here pile-driver crews are working day and night shifts in erecting dockage facilities at the mouth of Ship creek. A monster barge

Secretary Lane to Receive First Copy

Anchorage, Alaska, June 5, 1915

Hon. Franklin K. Lane,
Secretary of the Interior,
Washington, D. C.

Sir: The publishers of the Cook Inlet Pioneer wish to present to you the first copy of the first newspaper issued at Anchorage, Alaska, a prospective commercial center of importance, which owes its birth to the great Alaskan railway system now building from this point. We appreciate your wise efforts and achievements looking to-ward the development of our vast northern empire, so rich in natural resources and so sorely in need of the transport-ation facilities which the building of the government rail-way system will largely supply.

The Pioneer will make an effort to publish only trust-worthy information concerning the huge railway project, and knowing your interest in the matter, we are placing your name on our subscription list.

Respectfully,
COOK INLET PIONEER.

Business Firms and Individuals in Local Trade

Practically all kinds of essen-tial businesses are represented in Anchorage, and in making his rounds the Pioneer man gathered the names of the following:

In the general merchandise business are Brown & Hawkins, with J. W. Kempf in immediate charge, Finklestein & Sapiro, Carl W. Bolte, F. E. Parker and B. O. Tiedemann, A. Wilson, N. W. Pilger, E. H. Hertel, Wend-ler & Larson, Sheehan & Co., A. M. Laska, F. D. McCullough, Mrs. Walsh, J.M. Blase and John Bulaich & Co.

In the restaurant and bakery business are Mike Reilly, A. E. Dickson and Dave Mahoney,

Part of the first page of the first issue of the Cook Inlet Pioneer. Courtesy of Anchorage Historical and Fine Arts Museum

The Cook Inlet Pioneer *originated in June 1915 in the tent city as the weekly* Knik News *edited by L. F. Shaw. By the time of this September 10, 1915, picture at the new Anchorage quarters, the paper was published daily. It evolved into the Anchorage Daily Times. Courtesy of Pyatt Photo, Alaska Historical Library*

When the Crescent Hotel moved to the townsite, it first used this structure before building its two-story building on Fourth Avenue. Courtesy of Pyatt Collection, Alaska Historical Library

The Crescent was one of the first hotels built in the new townsite. It later became the Lane Hotel. The Alaska Hotel is now located on the upper floor of the same building on Fourth Avenue and C Street. Courtesy of Alaska Engineering Commission, Alaska Historical Library

"C" ST. HILL AND NEW FOOT BRIDGE.
SEPT. 30-16.

The Hotel Anchorage on Third Avenue is shown in an early stage of the building. The Anchorage developed into one of the leading hotels in the territory. Courtesy of Alaska Engineering Commission, Alaska Historical Library

Three ads from early editions of the Cook Inlet Pioneer. *Courtesy of the Anchorage Historical and Fine Arts Museum*

Fourth Avenue on November 10, 1915. The wide street was free of traffic and used only by some children and their dogs. This view was east from about E Street. Courtesy of Sydney Laurence Photo, Anchorage Historical and Fine Arts Museum

"Ladies Dog-team Race—Mrs. Casy James in the lead." This race along Fourth Avenue did not have to compete with heavy traffic in 1916. Courtesy of Pyatt Collection, Alaska Historical Library

Although the streets remained unpaved for many years, wide concrete sideways were laid along Fourth Avenue in 1916. Not only did they give the town a settled and prosperous look but they also were a welcome addition during the ice break-up the next spring. Courtesy of Alaska Engineering Commission, Alaska Historical Library

Two small businesses and their proprietors on Fourth Avenue. Courtesy of Pyatt Collection, Alaska Historical Library

The small businesses in town had lots of competition. Here two small "sandwich men" help promote trade. Courtesy of Pyatt Collection, Alaska Historical Library

Fourth Avenue had a permanent and prosperous look for the Fourth of July parade in 1916. Parades with floats and representatives of organized groups were welcome activities in the growing town. The Alaska Labor Union is shown here passing by the Brown and Hawkins store, the Montana Pool Room, and the B. C. Nichols store. Courtesy of Anchorage Historical and Fine Arts Museum

Joe Spenard sits at the wheel of his City Express Ford, probably decorated for the Labor Day parade on September 4, 1916. The sign on the hood reads "Northwestern due about 2 P.M." for those who wanted to meet the ship. Spenard homesteaded in the area that now is a community bearing his name. His homestead included a resort that was popular for many years. Courtesy of Anchorage Historical and Fine Arts Museum

A float in the Labor Day parade, September 4, 1916, carried signs promoting Matanuska Farms and Chickaloon Coal. It was hoped these would provide both an economic base for the development of Anchorage and much-needed freight for the railroad. The float was sponsored by the Anchorage Chamber of Commerce. Courtesy of Alaska Engineering Commission, Alaska Historical Library

The Benevolent Order of Elks, No. 1351, was organized in July 1915. Here the "Grand Lodge and Installation of Officers and Charter Members" were photographed in front of their large log building on Fourth Avenue. They later moved to the location between Third Avenue and Christensen Drive. Courtesy of Anchorage Historical and Fine Arts Museum

The cornerstone for the Masonic Temple was laid October 22, 1916, on Fourth Avenue. Courtesy of Alaska Engineering Commission, Alaska Historical Library

Masonic Lodge Number 221 was organized in February 1917. A Masons' float featuring a replica of a camel passes before the Masonic Temple in this photograph, probably taken during a Fourth of July celebration. The site has been used by Woolworth's since about 1962. Courtesy of Anchorage Historical and Fine Arts Museum

In the school children's parade on July 4, 1916, everyone wore their best clothes. In the center is Miss Orah Dee Clark, one of the first five teachers in Anchorage. She served as principal from the first school sessions in 1915 and retired as a teacher in 1944. Clark Junior High School was named for her. Courtesy of Anchorage Historical and Fine Arts Museum

The Pioneer School was built by the Alaska Engineering Commission in 1915. Anchorage Public School, the town's second school, shown here, was built in 1917 to house the growing student enrollments and was supplemented by a new high school in 1930. The second school was torn down in 1938 and replaced by Central Grade School, which later became the City Hall Annex. Courtesy of Cameron Collection, Archives, University of Alaska, Fairbanks

The 1918 first grade at the second school. Courtesy of Anchorage Historical and Fine Arts Museum

The Commercial Room at Anchorage Public School, 1918. Courtesy of Anchorage Historical and Fine Arts Museum

Seventh Grade. Public School. Anchorage, Alaska.

Seventh Grade, second school, 1918.
Courtesy of Anchorage Historical
and Fine Arts Museum

This 1915 log depot was replaced in 1916 by a frame building in the standard Alaska Engineering Commission style. Courtesy of Alaska Engineering Commission, Alaska Historical Library

The first train leaves the new depot—November 1, 1916. Courtesy of Alaska Engineering Commission, Alaska Historical Library

The Matanuska-Chickaloon train leaving Anchorage. Courtesy of Lulu Fairbanks Collection, Archives, University of Alaska, Fairbanks

This view of the terminal buildings was probably taken in 1917. The building in the distance on the right is the Pacific Grocery Company Wholesale. Courtesy of Alaska Engineering Commission, Alaska Historical Library

Frederick Mears, left, chairman and chief engineer of the Alaska Engineering Commission, and his staff are shown about 1917. Mears served as general manager of the Alaska Railroad from 1919 to 1923. To the left of Mears are C. L. Mason, chief clerk; William Gerig, assistant chief engineer; H. P. Warren, chief supply division; F. Hansen, engineer for maintenance and construction; and B. H. Barndollar, examiner of accounts and legal advisor. Courtesy of Anchorage Historical and Fine Arts Museum

City Hall, May Day, 1917. The city was incorporated November 23, 1920. Until that time, the Alaska Engineering Commission had managed the community through a townsite manager whose headquarters would have been in this building. The sign at the side door states "Dr. Benedict, Health Officer." Courtesy of Alaska Engineering Commission, Alaska Historical Library

Thomas Riggs was Governor of Alaska from 1918 to 1921. He came to Alaska with the gold rushes to Dawson and Nome. He was later chief engineer on the Alaska-Canada Boundary Commission. His association with Anchorage began with his membership on the Alaska Engineering Commission. Together with Frederick Mears and William C. Edes, the other Commission members, Riggs studied routes for the proposed railroad in 1914 from a headquarters camp at Ship Creek. Courtesy of Alaska Purchase Collection, Alaska Historical Library

The Delrosa unloading at the Alaska Engineering Commission dock. Courtesy of Anchorage Historical and Fine Arts Museum

"Carnation Milk, the Alaska Cow" was a comment on the use of canned milk in the new town. At Dock Number One a fifteen-ton derrick lifted materials from

barges. At low tide, barges could rest on a grid constructed next to the dock. Courtesy of Sydney Laurance Photo, Anchorage Historical and Fine Arts Museum

Locomotive cranes Number One and Number Two unload a spreader from the barge Lawrence, *June 13, 1917. Courtesy of Lulu Fairbanks Collection, Archives, University of Alaska, Fairbanks*

Alaska Engineering Commission Machine Shops, Marine Ways, May 1, 1919. The ways were used to store small ships in winter. The "mosquito fleet" served the communities and camps along the inlet. Courtesy of Alaska Engineering Commission, Alaska Historical Library

Winter at the shipways with barges and a small ship stored while ice builds up in the inlet. Courtesy of Alaska Railroad Collection, Alaska Historical Library

"A.E. Commission Cafeteria, Messhall and Dormitories 1, 2 and 3 June 8, 1919" Courtesy of Alaska Engineering Commission, Alaska Historical Library

In September, 1915, the Alaska Engineering Commission, which assumed responsibility for many services in the new townsite, began laying water lines. This rough building was the city water pumping station. Courtesy of Alaska Railroad Collection, Alaska Historical Library

The Alaska Engineering Commission Warehouse was one of a large complex of service buildings in the Ship Creek basin. Courtesy of Lulu Fairbanks Collection, Archives, University of Alaska, Fairbanks

The Alaska Engineering Commission provided various public services. Here is the telephone and telegraph building in 1918. Courtesy of Anchorage Historical and Fine Arts Museum

A YMCA for Alaska Engineering Commission employees was housed for many years in a log building that formerly had been used as the first hospital for the Alaska Engineering Commission. The "Rustlers" and the "Hustlers" were posed at the Administration Building after a membership drive in which the teams competed to enroll new members in the Railroad Department YMCA. The poster reads "30,000 New Members Wanted, Nov. 16 to 24, 1916." Courtesy of Alaska Engineering Commission, Alaska Historical Library

The Alaska Engineering Commission Mechanical Department poses with Engine Number 606 about 1918. Courtesy of Anchorage Historical and Fine Arts Museum

Anchorage Terminal Yards Fire Department. Courtesy of Alaska Engineering Commission, Alaska Historical Library

Although the streets remained unpaved for many years, wide concrete sidewalks were laid along Fourth Avenue in 1916. They gave a settled and prosperous look to the town and were a welcome addition during the break-up next spring. Courtesy of Alaska Engineering Commission, Alaska Historical Society

The U.S. Islander *was one of the "mosquito fleet" that provided services on the inlet. The sternwheeler at left has Matanuska printed across her side. Courtesy of Alaska Railroad Collection, Alaska Historical Library*

This photo is labeled: "Potter Creek 'Limited' Hansen-Ozone Parlor Car Service." Engines like this took work crews, and supplies to the Potter Creek camp. Courtesy of Alaska Railroad Collection, Alaska Historical Library

Potter Creek was one of the camps built for workers on the railroad south of Anchorage. This was Camp 101 of the Turnagain Arm Division. Courtesy of Alaska Railroad Collection, Alaska Historical Library

These cottages on Government Hill were built in 1915. Later, cottages were built in the townsite closer to the Alaska Engineering Commission headquarters and to the services of the town. Twelve of these houses still exist on Government Hill, although most have undergone some alteration. Courtesy of Alaska Engineering Commission, Alaska Historical Library

The Alaska Engineering Commission Hospital, located between Second and Third avenues just west of Barrow Street, was built to replace the original log Alaska Engineering Commission hospital at the base of Government Hill. The hospital and adjacent cottages were occupied by early 1917. In 1948 it became a dormitory for railway employees, and it was demolished in 1962. The site is now part of the approach to the overpass to Elmendorf Air Force Base. Courtesy of Alaska Engineering Commission, Alaska Historical Library

"U.S. Deputy Marshals destroying liquor. Anchorage, Alaska, June 30, 1917."

Anchorage was supposed to be a "dry" town. Voters had strongly supported Prohibition in the 1916 election. The Women's Christian Temperance Union was formally organized in October 1917, and Mrs. Robert Lee Hatcher, whose husband mined in the Willow Creek area, was a prominent leader in the movement. The marshal's office was kept busy hunting down illegal stills and liquor operations. A note on the back of this photo says: "The law is being strictly enforced in most towns. One year in jail and a heavy fine is the sentence that is usually imposed on any man who is caught with liquor in his possession or on his premises." Courtesy of Anchorage Historical and Fine Arts Museum

...RSHALS DISTROYING LIQUOR.
...GE, ALASKA, JUNE 30-17.

The first draft for military service for World War I took place on Fourth Avenue near the Jack Robards building. This is probably May 1917. The war slowed down railroad construction. Courtesy of Anchorage Historical and Fine Arts Museum

During the Labor Day parade, September 3, 1917, a Red Cross ambulance passes the Masonic Temple at the southwest corner of Fourth Avenue and F Street. Businesses and offices were housed on the lower floors. The words on the ambulance sign are "Join Now." An agricultural fair is being held in the lot next door; its sign reads "Welcome." The three-windowed building at the center left in the picture is Robards Hall, which offered bowling and pool on the ground floor and a dance floor above. Next is Eckman's store, then the Bon Marche. A Carrol and Company float is passing in front of the Bon Marche. Courtesy of Anchorage Historical and Fine Arts Museum

The Red Cross, officially organized in August 1917, became very active in the war effort. Here, the Ladies Red Cross Auxiliary (May 25, 1918) attended the Red Cross Benefit baseball game between the Masons and the Elks. Identified in the picture are Mrs. Roberts, second from left; Mrs. Chase, fourth from left; and Edith Danton, third from right. Mrs. Moyer is in the window. Courtesy of Anchorage Historical and Fine Arts Museum

The Masons and Elks baseball team were well equipped for the Red Cross Benefit baseball game on May 25, 1918. The reason the Elks are wearing mortarboards was not explained. Courtesy of Anchorage Historical and Fine Arts Museum

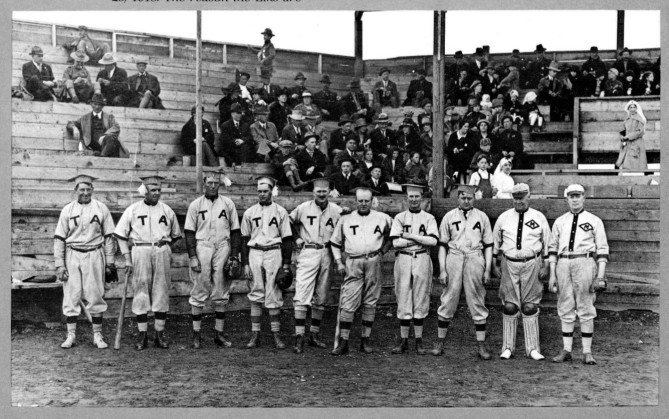

In a parade honoring "recruits," held on June 30, 1918, the men marched past the City Hall on Fourth Avenue. The Anchorage Times building can be seen beyond the field. Courtesy of Alaska Engineering Commission, Alaska Historical Library

Because Anchorage was strongly affected by World War I, the service on Fourth Avenue on "Decoration Day" May 30, 1918, attracted a crowd. Courtesy of Alaska Engineering Commission, Alaska Historical Library

"Hauling $650,000 in bullion from the Iditarod. Anchorage, Alaska, Jan. 4th, 1917." The early trail from Iditarod to Seward by this time used Anchorage as its terminus. The fame of the route is still commemorated in the annual dog race from Anchorage to Nome. Courtesy of Sydney Laurence Photo, Anchorage Historical and Fine Arts Museum

These men, on a warm day (note the open transom), are admiring a $10,800 gold display. This was a two-week run from the Fern Mine in the Willow Creek District. Anchorage quickly became the center for handling and shipping gold from the Iditarod, Willow, Hope, and Sunshine mining areas. Courtesy of Lulu Fairbanks Collection, Archives, University of Alaska, Fairbanks

This photo is labeled "Funeral of First Shooting Scrape in Anchorage, July 9th, 1916." Alex Takoff, the victim, was shot by Sam Casoff on Fourth Avenue on July 6 in revenge for a murdered brother. According to the Anchorage Times both men were "Russians" and the brother's murder had taken place before the men came to the United States. Courtesy of Sydney Laurence Company Photo, Anchorage Historical and Fine Arts Museum

"The funeral of Ernest Podboy under the auspices of Igloo No. 15 Pioneers of Alaska. At Anchorage. May 12, 1918." In this photo by Basil Clemons, the flag in the background flies at half-mast. The building to the right is Anchorage's second school. Courtesy of Harry DeVone Collection, Archives, University of Alaska, Fairbanks

89

The Chamber of Commerce was organized in 1915 with J. H. Smith and Anthony J. Wendler as its first presidents. The window displays mineral specimens and sheaves of grain, symbolic of their hopes for a prosperous future based on mining and agriculture. The sign on the window identifies A. S. Koch as secretary. That may be him in the doorway. Courtesy of Anchorage Historical and Fine Arts Museum

The early days of railroad construction were affected by labor problems, mainly relating to wages. The Alaska Labor Union was a strong force in dealing with the Alaska Engineering Commission. Their building was located on the block bounded by Seventh and Eighth avenues between G and H streets. Courtesy of Pyatt Collection, Alaska Historical Library

The Bank of Alaska started with these modest premises but has grown to be one of the major financial institutions in the state. This small building was at Fourth Avenue and E Street. Courtesy of Anchorage Historical and Fine Arts Museum

A sign on the trail to Seward advertises some of the businesses in the new town site. Courtesy of Anchorage Historical and Fine Arts Museum

The turret on the Larson and Wendler building made it unique in Anchorage. The Wendlers lived on the second floor and continued the business after Larson left it. The building has remained in the family and today is a restaurant run by Mrs. Myrtle (Wendler) Stalnaker, the daughter of A. J. Wendler. The building has undergone changes in style as well as uses but remains distinctly recognizable. Courtesy of Alaska Engineering Commission, Alaska Historical Library

The Carrol Building was one of the important business establishments in the new town. Sydney Laurence had his photography studio in the building when it first opened. The building still exists at 434 and 435 Fourth Avenue, although the peaked false front is gone and the facade remodeled. This 1915 float carried the motto "On our soul we put your uppers." The large building next door was the Byrne's Building. At the time of this photo it was used as a movie theatre. Courtesy of Anchorage Historical and Fine Arts Museum

The 1917 Labor Day parade featured a prominent float for Carrol and Company, Men's Outfitters with George, Freda, and Ted Carrol on the left. At the right is Ike Coleman, who worked for the company and was also the catcher for the Anchorage baseball team. Courtesy of Anchorage Historical and Fine Arts Museum

The interior of Carrol's store was photographed by Sydney Laurence, probably in 1916. The well-stocked, dimly lit establishment had a large barrel stove as the main source of heat. Electricity was provided through the Alaska Engineering Commission power plant in 1916. Courtesy of Anchorage Historical and Fine Arts Museum

The Lathrop Building at 801 West Fourth Avenue was one of the largest of the early buildings. The first floor was built in 1915; the second story was added in 1916. Mrs. T. D. Corlew, the first tenant, offered "dry goods, shoes, and ladies furnishings." The Alaska Steamship Company had its offices on H Street. Since then, many other businesses have occupied the building, although its appearance has been changed by the removal of the cornices and the addition of new siding.

Built by Captain Austin E. Lathrop, a leading business leader in Alaska, this building predated the early Empress Theatre and the imposing Fourth Avenue Theatre that were only two in a chain of theatres he developed across Alaska. Courtesy of Anchorage Historical and Fine Arts Museum

When the Empress Theatre opened on July 1, 1916, the feature was Peggy with Billy Burke, and admission was one dollar. Modern and attractive, the Empress provided most of the amenities of theatres in larger·communities in the United States and was one of the earliest concrete structures in Alaska. The main feature when this photo was taken was Gates of Eden with Viola Dana. Courtesy of Alaska Engineering Commission, Alaska Historical Library

The interior of the Empress Theatre was ornately outfitted with a fine stage, a screen, and both an organ and a piano to accompany performances. Courtesy of Alaska Engineering Commission, Alaska Historical Library

John M. Reid, Lawyer, occupied this building. He is not identified in this group of men, but the stools seem to indicate this was a regular gathering place. Courtesy of Pyatt Collection, Alaska Historical Library

Log buildings like this small residence were, and are today typical of Alaska and many northern areas. Courtesy of Cameron Collection, Archives, University of Alaska, Fairbanks

The movie theatre in the Byrne's Building was replaced by Sam Shucklin's men's store about 1917. By now new concrete sidewalks were in, and this part of the business area looked attractive and prosperous. Courtesy of Anchorage Historical and Fine Arts Museum

In 1915, Emerelda McDonald (Mrs. P. J.) posed in front of their house on the corner of F Street and Fifth Avenue. While the simple frame house was typical of many built in the new town, the McDonalds' frame and wire fence was a distinctive feature. Courtesy of Anchorage Historical and Fine Arts Museum

94

This large house with eight rooms was located just below Christensen Drive at 750 Second Avenue. It was built by the Alaska Engineering Commission for Commissioner Mears, whose family moved in about February 1917; the garage was added in 1928. Mrs. Mears held an "at home" every Wednesday from 2 to 5 p.m. Later, the house became known as the Ohlson house after the last Alaska Railroad general manager to occupy it. Photographed in the 1930s, the buildings were razed in 1973. Courtesy of Anchorage Historical and Fine Arts Museum

This imposing house was built for Judge Leopold David in 1917. It still stands at 605 West Second Avenue and looks today very much as it did then. David came to Alaska in 1904 with the army and later lived in Seward and Knik. He came to Ship Creek in 1915 and served as United States Commissioner and District Recorder. He served as mayor of Anchorage for three terms starting on November 29, 1920. Courtesy of Anchorage Historical and Fine Arts Museum

The U.S. Commissioners office about 1920. Anna David and her daughter, Caroline, stand in front of the building which was located at 5th and E, now the site of the National Bank of Alaska building. Courtesy of Anchorage Historical and Fine Arts Museum

An open air patriotic and religious service in 1918 drew a crowd while the Anchorage City Band performed. Courtesy of Anchorage Historical and Fine Arts Museum

Anchorage was a stable town where many churches were built as the community grew. This was the Congregational Church congregation about 1918. Courtesy of Anchorage Historical and Fine Arts Museum

This agricultural fair welcomed people on September 3-5, 1917. The elaborate entrance led to booths and activities. Courtesy of Anchorage Historical and Fine Arts Museum

Baseball was popular in early Anchorage, and enthusiastic participants included Mrs. Ramsey, sliding into home plate, and Mrs. Dickson, catching. The bleachers and backstop in this 1917 photograph were located in the Park Strip area at Ninth and C streets. Courtesy of Anchorage Historical and Fine Arts Museum

Anchorage Fire Department Headquarters, August 16, 1919. Courtesy of Lulu Fairbanks Collection, Archives, University of Alaska, Fairbanks

Federal Buildings Anchorage-Alaska   Cameron 364

The post office, the telephone and telegraph building, and the federal jail (left to right) were located on a site known as the Federal Reserve. This view is looking west at the north side of Fourth Avenue. The Federal Building, built in 1939, now occupies the site. Courtesy of Cameron Collection, Archives, University of Alaska, Fairbanks

The 1917 fair included a baby show which brought out handsome children and proud mothers with a few impressive perambulators. Eighth from the right is Mrs. Peter Sundberg, with her grandson, Jack Wilson; third from the right is Mrs. Fred McCutchen; sixth from the right is Mrs. Jessie Parsons holding her son, Stanley. Courtesy of Anchorage Historical and Fine Arts Museum

Excursion of Anchorage baseball fans to Potter Creek. July 1, 1917. The passengers in their best clothes crowded into dump cars for the run. Courtesy of Alaska Engineering Commission, Alaska Historical Library

A birthday party at the Two Girls Cafe. The Koslosky children, the Baylis girls, Ted and Freda Carrol, and Gerard Shucklin were among those present on this special occasion. Courtesy of Anchorage Historical and Fine Arts Museum

Chapter Five

The Incorporated Town:

1920-1940

A cannery on the dock near the mouth of Ship Creek. The boat is the Whitworth, *out of Seattle. Commercial cannery operations began in the 1920s. This appears to be the General Fish Company. Emards Packing Company was the other major cannery. Its facilities were later used by the Whitney-Fidalgo Company. Courtesy of Anchorage Historical and Fine Arts Museum*

By 1920 the five years of Commission management of Anchorage ended. The citizens of Anchorage, comfortable with federal paternalism, were reluctant to assume full responsibility for their own affairs; but, after considerable pressure, they voted to incorporate the town and to elect a city council. On November 23, 1920, the district judge declared Anchorage to be incorporated. The men of the Commission, within five years, had fashioned a modern community in a wilderness setting. To accomplish this, they had worked with sometimes-balky officials, dealt with inadequate laws and regulations, and suffered much local criticism. In summary, their achievements were remarkable.

There was excitement in southcentral Alaska in 1923 when President Warren G. Harding planned to visit the north—the first time a chief executive had visited the territory during his term of office. Alaskans looked upon the visit as an opportunity to present their views to the president on a variety of matters, including the administrative tangle which existed in Alaska, where five cabinet officers and twenty-eight bureaus exercised authority. The president also planned to drive the traditional golden spike which signified the completion of the Alaska Railroad.

While the 1920s, with the exception of agriculture, were a period of prosperity for the United States, Alaska, not really in the mainstream of American life, was little affected. The segments of the American economy that prospered were related to manufacturing and commerce, but salmon and gold were Alaska's chief exports, and a substantial number of Alaskans provided most of their needs for themselves. The twenties, however, witnessed the beginnings of the air age, a development that would have a profound effect on the territory, and particularly on Anchorage.

There were probably few places on earth which needed air transportation more than Alaska. Much of the interior and arctic were still unmapped, and Alaskan towns and settlements were isolated from each other and the States by nearly impassable mountains, pathless plains of tundra snowcovered in the winter, and innumerable lakes, streams, and rivers. In fact, the sea offered the only exit.

Reputedly, it was James V. Martin who shipped the first plane to Alaska—a small tractor biplane which he had delivered to Fairbanks and assembled there for a Fourth of July exhibition in 1913. He made four flights that day.

By 1922, Fourth Avenue had become a commercial street with few residences remaining along the main blocks. Its broad street, wide sidewalks, and variety of businesses could compare favorably with most American towns of its size at that time. A feature which set Anchorage apart then and which continues to enhance its appearance is the scenic view of the mountains to the east and of the inlet to the west. Courtesy of Anchorage Historical and Fine Arts Museum

Locals were impressed with the flying machine. A few years later, the Army's Black Wolf Squadron of four open-cockpit De Havillands arrived in Nome after flying across the United States and Canada, surviving numerous forced landings and minor crashes along the way. And in 1921, a daredevil named Clarence Prest tried to fly a Curtiss Jenny named *Polar Bear* through Alaska to Siberia to collect a $25,000 prize offered by a movie producer to the first pilot to make the flight. He crashed on Prince Rupert Island, but tried again in 1922, flying an OX-5 Standard, christened *Polar Bear II*. He made it as far as Eagle on the Yukon River, but crashed for the fifth and final time of the trip near the Seventy Mile River. Abandoning the plane, Prest hiked out to civilization.

Alaskan bush pilots soon pioneered northern flying, and successfully tied together a geographically diverse and difficult territory.

Anchorage citizens recognized the importance of aviation, and by 1923 the town boasted of an airport. In 1925 Russell Merrill, an ex-Navy pilot, arrived in Alaska. By 1927 Merrill, G. E. "Ed" Young, and Lyle Stanford were the three pilots of the newly created Anchorage Air Transports Company which provided the first commercial airline service. Merrill scored a host of first achievements. He was the first to cross the Alaska Range and the first to fly over the remote Kuskokwim area on November 8, 1927. Unable to fly through Rainy Pass because of bad weather, he probed further to the south and discovered a second pass which was later named in his honor. Merrill Field, just outside of Anchorage, also commemorates his name. Merrill left Anchorage on the afternoon of September 16, 1929, to deliver a compressor to a gold mine. He failed to reach his destination, and his wreck was never found. A piece of fabric which washed ashore on Cook Inlet was identified by mechanics who had worked on his plane.

The military had long recognized Alaska's importance as a base for aerial operations, and in the summer of 1927 the Army Air Corps sent a group to Anchorage to make a reconnaissance of flying conditions. Seven years later, on August 2, 1934, ten army bombers under the command of Lieutenant-Colonel H. H. Arnold landed at Anchorage's Merrill Field on another reconnaissance mission. But it took Adolf Hitler's invasion of Norway and Denmark on April 9, 1940, to persuade many congressmen that the Scandinavian Peninsula was just over the top of the earth from Alaska and that bombers able to fly such a distance existed. That same year, construction of an air base four miles from Anchorage began.

In 1945 Merrill Field still had all the appearances of a frontier airport. A modern control tower stood out among a row of wooden hangars and shacks. But the runway in that year was one of the busiest in America. In one month in 1945, Merrill Field recorded 10,000 landings and take-offs, more civilian operations than logged by LaGuardia Field, New York in a comparable month in that same year.

In short, the airplane quickly became the Alaskan mode of transportation, tying together communities which normally would have been completely isolated because of their remoteness. By the 1960s Anchorage had become the refueling point for most international airlines flying the transpolar route.

In the meantime, Alaska's population grew slowly. While the territory had a total population of 55,036 in 1920, the figure had grown to a modest 59,278 in 1930. Anchorage had counted 1,856 residents in 1920 and registered a modest increase in 1930 with a count of 2,736.

Doris Walkowski, a long-time resident who came north in 1926, remembers her busy life in early Anchorage. She left Seattle on the S.S. *Northwestern* and landed in Seward, from where she took the train to Anchorage. There had been terrific forest fires in the town's vicinity, and the air was a hazy brown through which a red sun shone. It was a small town, with many wooden sidewalks, and one could hear the thump, thump of approaching footsteps for blocks away. There were few single women. She had met her future husband on the ship coming north, and three months later, at the age of seventeen, she was engaged to him, and married three years later, in 1929, after he had finished his university training.

Doris Walkowski worked for the First National Bank, and in her spare time went skiing, hiking, and ice skating out in Spenard. There also existed opportunities for playing tennis, and Anchorage even possessed a nine-hole golf course. Silent movies were well attended, and the Saturday night dances at the Elks drew large crowds.

Alaskans were avid card players, and bridge in particular was very popular. It was not long before Doris Walkowski joined one of the many bridge clubs. She also had to fashion for herself a

By October 21, 1921, the mouth of Ship Creek had changed a great deal. Buildings, docks, and ships gave the area a built-up appearance that foreshadowed the modern

suitable wardrobe, consisting of three long dresses, to take advantage of the many social events. Mail arrived once a week, and a small library furnished adequate reading materials. In fact, life was never dull.

The Alaska Railroad continued to be the mainstay of Anchorage's economy despite the uneven appropriations Congress provided for its operation and maintenance. Frederick Mears, who had left Alaska at the outbreak of the war to serve in France, returned after the conflict for a four-year term as general manager of the railroad. He left that position in 1923 at the time of the Alaska Road Commission-Alaska Railroad merger, for the president of the road organization served as the head of both organizations.

industrial and commercial area in the Ship Creek Basin. Courtesy of Anchorage Historical and Fine Arts Museum

on its $70 million investment. Howell stated that the railroad had lost money and was losing more, and that its revenue was declining. More importantly, it had not fulfilled its intent for developing Alaska's economy, and it was doubtful that it would do so in the near future.

The sharp increases in revenues brought protests from Alaskans, and many merchants and travelers took as much of the freight and passenger business as possible to the railroad's competition. Buses and trucks on the Richardson Highway, gasoline boats from Seattle to Cook Inlet, and airplanes—all claimed more and more tourists, business travelers, and high value freight. Steamers to Saint Michael at the mouth of the Yukon River carried fuel. Competition and increasing effects of the Great Depression lowered revenues far below the expectations of the Howell Committee. Not only did revenues decrease significantly but also there was a net loss of revenue tonnage from 101,470 in 1931 to 97,479 in 1933.

As the Depression deepened, Alaska, although not suffering as much from the trauma as were the States, was not entirely unaffected. Employment in the fishing and mining industries declined. Eventually, Alaskans shared in President Franklin Delano Roosevelt's New Deal, but because Alaska was a territory and not a state, its share of federal funds and programs was often small.

Lorene Harrison came to Alaska and Anchorage for the first time in 1928 to teach school. After a stint of teaching, she left, but returned in 1934. This was the height of the Depression in the States, but as soon as she and her husband got on the northbound ship in Seattle, the ever pervasive talk of the Depression ceased. Once in Anchorage, her husband got a job with the Alaska Railroad, one he kept until after the end of World War II. The couple rented a house which featured a coal burning kitchen range and a wood burning stove in the front room. In the fall, the men went hunting and usually shot a moose or two. Cleaned and quartered, the meat was hung on the back porch where it stayed frozen all winter long. They caught plenty of salmon which they froze and canned in big pressure cookers. Most families had large vegetable gardens with cabbage, cauliflower, radishes, potatoes, and turnips, among others, and the women picked wild berries to further supplement the diet. Families

Colonel James Gordon Steese was manager for six months, but the consolidated operations of railroad and road commission soon ceased. The problems of the railroad were overwhelming, and maintenance and repair problems were extensive. After several changes in managers, Colonel Otto F. Ohlson became general manager of the railroad in 1928.

With continuing rail deficits, Congress applied heavy pressure for drastic economies, and in August 1931 the Special Select Committee on Investigation of the Alaska Railroad arrived in the territory. This committee, named after its chairman Senator Robert B. Howell of Nebraska, recommended drastic increases in freight and passenger rates in order to permit a fair return

By the 1920s Alaska had become a tourist destination. Here a group of "round trippers" arrive on the S.S. Alameda on July 14, 1923. Courtesy of Anchorage Historical and Fine Arts Museum

In the 1920s, the government hospital on the hill and the depot in the foreground were important landmarks in Anchorage. The vehicle at the depot transported rail

cut their own firewood, and taken all together, it took relatively little cash for the Harrisons and other Depression era residents to get by in Anchorage.

And although the territory did not benefit as fully from various actions taken by the New Deal administration, several programs were helpful to Alaska. The president's decision to devalue the dollar by raising the price of gold to thirty-five dollars an ounce stimulated employment in the ailing gold mining industry. Direct relief payments also aided individuals and helped the economy. The Works Project Administration provided employment, and the Public Works Administration sponsored a variety of projects in which private contractors employed men and women at the prevailing wage in the community. As a result of their efforts, a number of public buildings and bridges were constructed;

a guidebook to Alaska was published; harbors were improved, and a hotel was built at Mount McKinley National Park along the railroad. In addition, those enrolled in the Civilian Conservation Corps received a dollar a day plus board and room while they built roads and trails in the national forests, planted trees, and worked on other reforestation projects.

However, of all the New Deal activities in Alaska, the Matanuska Valley Colony excited the greatest interest, extending far beyond the boundaries of the territory. One of many

106

*Bob Bragaw and Ira Losey were
Alaskan guides in the 1920s. This
was one of their camps in McKinley
Park, appearing comfortable and
well equipped. The equipment is
hardly lightweight; imagine carrying
those tentpoles around! Courtesy of
Anchorage Historical and Fine Arts
Museum*

resettlement projects under the Roosevelt administration, this was designed to take people away from rural districts, in which poverty had been prevalent long before the Depression, and to move them into areas where they might lead more productive lives. No other settlement received as much publicity as Matanuska, for the idea of creating a community in the wilderness stirred many imaginations. Expectations were high. Officials of the Alaska Railroad, who had long sponsored Alaskan railbelt settlement, were delighted because this meant that the federal government was doing something for the territory. Last, but not least, many believed that such a colony would clearly demonstrate the feasibility of farming in the north and consequently that successful agriculture would help to free Alaska from dependence on the outside for supplies.

Matanuska eventually receded from the front pages, but Anchorage remained in the public eye. Economic revival in the states affected Alaska as well, and residents of Anchorage were optimistic as the 1930s drew to a close. Many people began to build substantial homes. The Alaska Railroad benefitted from the economic upsurge as well, and slowly, Colonel Ohlson put the line into the black. Both freight and passenger revenues rose year by year from 1934 through 1939. In short, there was promise of economic well being in the 1940s.

*One of the features of the Fourth
of July celebration in 1920 was a
seven-mile marathon race. Here, the
four participants are ready to start.
The winner was the man with his
arms folded. The starter was
George E. Pollar. Courtesy of
Anchorage Historical and Fine Arts
Museum*

*During his visit, Warren G. Harding
took the throttle of engine 618 for a
twenty-six-mile run to Willow. Mrs.
Harding rode in the cab with him.
Engineer Brayford stood beside
Harding, and Herbert Hoover,
secretary of commerce, was behind
the cab.*

*The president and his party,
traveling on the navel vessel
Henderson, had left Tacoma on
July 6, 1923. A week later the party
arrived in Anchorage and received
an enthusiastic welcome. After
spending three hours in the town,
the party boarded the train for
Wasilla and Nenana, where the
president drove the golden spike.
After a visit to Fairbanks, he
returned by train to Anchorage
where, after a short inspection of
Lake Spenard and a visit to the
Elk's Hall, the party continued to
Seward. Courtesy of Alaska Historical Library*

Florence Kling De Wolfe (Mrs. Warren G.) Harding, during the 1923 presidential visit, posed with James G. Steese, who had just become the Chairman and Chief Engineer of the Alaska Engineering Commission. Previously, president of the Alaska Road Commission, Steese assumed the Alaska Engineering Commission duties when the organizations were temporarily combined. Courtesy of Alaska Historical Library

President Warren G. Harding came to Alaska in July 1923 to drive the golden spike that symbolized the completion of the Alaska Railroad. The ceremony took place on the north bank of the Tanana at Nenana on a hot July 15. Mrs. Harding is in a long dress and large hat, and Herbert Hoover stands just to her right. Courtesy of Lulu Fairbanks Collection, Archives, University of Alaska, Fairbanks

A fire on Fourth Avenue February 7, 1922, attracted open cars on the street as well as a horse-drawn sleigh. The goods piled in the street may have been a precaution against loss if the fire spread. The Anchorage Daily Times *reported: "Fire originating in the kitchen of the Royal Cafe at 9:05 this morning caused a property loss of approximately $50,000." All the businesses in the block were affected in some way. Volunteers used two hoses and impartially switched them from building to building. Brown and Hawkins' big store was saved. The 21st Infantry sent soldiers to guard the merchandise in the streets. Courtesy of Anchorage Historical and Fine Arts Museum*

Billy Butts' Ice Cream Parlor and Reception Hall was the location for this gathering of fashionable ladies. Courtesy of Anchorage Historical and Fine Arts Museum

Fraternal organizations played an important part in the community. Here, the Masonic Temple, built in 1917, stands next to the Oddfellows hall, completed in 1923. The lower floors were occupied by Gordons Department Store and the Bank of Anchorage. Courtesy of Lulu Fairbanks Collection, Archives, University of Alaska, Fairbanks

The Parsonage and Presbyterian Church stood along a gravel road about 1920. A chapel and reading room were located on F Street as early as 1915. A new church was dedicated on Tenth Avenue in 1968. Courtesy of Cameron Collection, Archives, University of Alaska, Fairbanks

The congregation celebrated the fifth anniversary of All Saints Episcopal Church on May 7, 1922. The simple building had many attractive features such as the windows with fanlights and the details of the covered porch. Courtesy of Anchorage Historical and Fine Arts Museum

The Presbyterian Sunday School float for the July 4, 1920, parade featured flowers, flags, and children in their Sunday best. Courtesy of Anchorage Historical and Fine Arts Museum

This circa 1924 aerial view shows a young city, with plenty of room in its original townsite. Snow on the roads and some roofs emphasizes the rigid layout of the townsite. The Park Strip, on the left, was cleared for use as an aviation field. The railway terminal buildings are clustered in the Ship Creek Basin at right. Courtesy of Anchorage Historical and Fine Arts Museum

Ninth Street was the last and farthest point south of the original townsite streets. The area beyond was first cleared as a firebreak to protect the townsite. Later it was improved for use as the municipal airfield. Over the years it has been known as the Park Strip and now is called Delaney Park after James J. Delaney, who was mayor of Anchorage for three terms from 1929 to 1931. Today, the strip still serves as an attractive break in the city fabric and is used by many people through all of the seasons. Courtesy of Anchorage Historical and Fine Arts Museum

During the 1920s, this house at 727 L Street was the home of Charlie Bisell, a pattern worker at the railroad foundry. The house was known for a long time as the J. Vic Brown house since Brown bought the house in 1934 and lived there for about twenty years. It was typical of many comfortable and attractive houses close to the business area. Brown was a jeweler in Anchorage who also had stores in other cities. Courtesy of Anchorage Historical and Fine Arts Museum

Aviation Field—Anchorage, Alaska

Anchorage Air Transports, Inc. Anchorage No. 1 *flew from the Park Strip. Courtesy of Anchorage Historical and Fine Arts Museum*

In June 1924 Noel Wien brought a crated J-One from Seward on the railroad. Wien and his mechanic, W. B. Yunker, assembled the plane and flew it from the aviation field, which had been cleared the year before by enthusiastic and hard-working townspeople. Wien flew the plane July 5, 1924, to Fairbanks along the railroad, marking the first Anchorage to Fairbanks flight. Courtesy of Anchorage Historical and Fine Arts Museum

Nellie Brown worked at the Brown homestead in 1924. Courtesy of Anchorage Historical and Fine Arts Museum

After Jack Brown left the Forest Service, he worked for the Alaska Engineering Commission. He and Nellie Brown homesteaded in the Government Hill area on what is now Elmendorf Air Force Base. Their homestead is shown in 1922. Courtesy of Anchorage Historical and Fine Arts Museum

Russell Merrill and his Travelair 7000 J-4 on the tidal flats near Anchorage. Courtesy of Anchorage Historical and Fine Arts Museum

Russell Merrill, a promising young pilot, was lost in a flight over Cook Inlet in 1929. In 1930 the Anchorage Women's Club proposed that the new airfield, (Anchorage's first field was the Park Strip), be named after Merrill. The field was dedicated as Merrill Field after approval by the City Council. The dedication plaque is now on the new tower. Courtesy of Anchorage Historical and Fine Arts Museum

J. J. Delaney, mayor from 1929 to 1931, was proud of his apple blossoms in 1926. The tree grew at 303 K Street Courtesy of Anchorage Historical and Fine Arts Museum

Mount McKinley was a favorite subject of Sydney Laurence. He painted it in many views and in many moods. Courtesy of University of Alaska Museum

Sydney Laurence, perhaps Alaska's best-known artist, made Anchorage his home for twenty-five years. He opened a photographic company in the Carrol Building from 1915 through 1916. When he returned to painting, he made his residence and studio in the Anchorage Hotel, which later evolved into the Westward Hilton. Laurence was known for his paintings of Mount McKinley in many moods. Examples of his work may be seen in the Anchorage Historical and Fine Arts Museum. This 1928 photograph by Nellie Brown shows Laurence with his new automobile. Courtesy of Anchorage Historical and Fine Arts Museum

Colonel Otto F. Ohlson was the general manager of the Alaska Railroad from 1928 to 1945. Here he is shown with his DeSoto sedan which was equipped to run on the railroad tracks. The Curry Hotel was a railroad facility where passengers could stay overnight on the run from Anchorage to Fairbanks.

A native of Sweden, Ohlson had worked as a superintendent for the Northern Pacific Railway before coming to Alaska. He believed in strict economy and one-man control of the railroad. During his tenure of more than seventeen years, he was considered a hard worker and a conscientious manager who was fair to his employees. During his stewardship, Ohlson made efforts to promote and to develop Alaska and to generate traffic for the railroad. Courtesy of Anchorage Historical and Fine Arts Museum

The Anchorage High School was built in 1930 on the south side of the school reserve. The auditorium was added to it at a later date.

Courtesy of Lulu Fairbanks Collection, Archives, University of Alaska, Fairbanks

The Anchorage Lumber and Construction Company was one of several building supply firms serving a growing community.

Courtesy of Kay Kennedy Collection, Archives, University of Alaska, Fairbanks

The Anchorage High School Orchestra of 1930–31 was a small group. Ken Laughlin was the organizer and director and the school system's first music supervisor. In the front row, from left to right. are: Leo Sorrela, Myrtle Flechenstein, "Tony" Antoinette H. Peterson, and Paul Howe. In the back row, one of the two young men on the left is "Heine" Swanson, the other is unidentified. Third from the left is Laughlin, then Bill Harriman. Courtesy of Anchorage Historical and Fine Arts Museum

A snowstorm in 1934 tied up Fourth Avenue. This view looking east shows the present site of the old Federal Building on the left and the old frame City Hall, just beyond the large drifts, on the right. Courtesy of Anchorage Historical and Fine Arts Museum

A reconnaissance group was sent to Alaska in 1929 before Lieutenant Colonel Arnold and his bomber squadron arrived on a map-and-survey mission in 1934. One of the group's planes went down on the mud flats but was recovered to fly again. Courtesy of Brigadier General Ross G. Hoyt Collection, Office of History, Alaskan Air Command, USAF Photo

The Central Grade School of 1939 (which later became the City Hall Annex) on Fifth and C was a Public Works Administration project. The project caused an interesting conflict between the Alaska Railroad and the city when Colonel Otto Ohlson, then manager, blocked supplies from getting to the site over a dispute concerning the city dock. Courtesy of Lulu Fairbanks Collection, Archives, University of Alaska, Fairbanks

Anchorage has always been in an ideal location for winter sports. Here is a slalom contest at the Winter Sports Tournament in February 1937. Courtesy of Archives, University of Alaska, Fairbanks

A high jump at the 1937 tournament. Courtesy of Lulu Fairbanks Collection, Archives, University of Alaska, Fairbanks

Star Air Service started in Anchorage about 1932 then merged with McGee Airways in 1934 to become Star Airlines. That company merged with several others to become Alaska Star Airlines, which dropped the "Star" from its name in 1944. Courtesy of Alaska Historical Library

During the summer of 1934, Lt. Col. Henry "Hap" Arnold led a flight of ten B-10 bombers from Bolling Field near Washington, D.C., to Alaska on a map-and-survey mission of Alaska. Six years later, another B-10 landed at Merrill Field, Anchorage Municipal Airport. Its crew included Maj. Everett S. Davis, S.Sgt. Joseph A. Grady, and Capt. Edward D. Smith. This was a forerunner of what was to become the Alaskan Air Command.

Front row, left to right: Capt. John D. Corkille, Capt. Harold M. McClelland, Capt. Ray A. Dunn, Capt. Westside T. Larson, Lt. Ralph A. Snavely, Lt. Nathan F. Twining, Lt. John S. Mills, Lt. Hez McClellan. Second row: Lt. Lawrence J. Carr, Lt. Charles B. Howard, Maj. Malcom C. Grow, Maj. Hugh J. Knerr, Lt. Col. Henry H. Arnold, Maj. Ralph Royce, Lt. John S. Griffith, Lt. Leonard F. Harman. Lt. Twining and Lt. Mills (alternates) did not go on flight. Courtesy of Office of History, Alaskan Air Command, USAF Photo

This float in the Fourth of July parade in 1932 won a fifteen dollar prize for Mrs. Walter Muller. The young women are identified as Betty on the left in red, Lilian in white, and Francis on the right in blue. Courtesy of Anchorage Historical and Fine Arts Museum

There was still a lot of work to be done when the Matanuska colonists arrived. Many lived temporarily in a tent city in Palmer in the spring of 1935—faintly reminiscent of Anchorage twenty years before. Courtesy of Lulu Fairbanks Collection, Archives, University of Alaska, Fairbanks

After coming to Alaska in 1896,
Captain Austin E. Lathrop settled in
Anchorage and worked in various
areas. He developed a chain of
movie theatres, including the
Empress and Fourth Avenue
theatres in Anchorage; radio
stations; and the Healy River Coal
Corporation which provided coal to
both Anchorage and Fairbanks.
Here he is shown at the Fairbanks
Railroad Station in 1930 with Lulu
Fairbanks (on the right), a journalist,
and Eva McGown, who for many
years served as hostess for the city.
Lathrop died in an accident at the
Healy Mine at age eighty-four, July
26, 1950. Courtesy of Anchorage
Historical and Fine Arts Museum

The Matanuska Colony project was expected to boost both the railroad and the economy of Anchorage. Two hundred and three families from northern counties of Michigan, Minnesota, and Wisconsin were greeted with dinners, speeches, and general fanfare on their way to their new home in the Valley in 1935. The town of Palmer became the center for the colony, which eventually brought thousands of acres under cultivation, built roads, and introduced modern agriculture to the area. This view of the post office and general store was taken in the mid-1930s. John Walsh, a carpenter's helper, is in the foreground. Courtesy of Lulu Fairbanks Collection, Archives, University of Alaska, Fairbanks

Chapter Six

Years
of
Transition:

1940-1960

The interior of the Federal Court House in 1938. The courtroom had not changed much since it was constructed soon after the move to the new townsite. Demands for a new facility, supported by Anthony J. Dimond, Territorial Delegate to Congress, led to the construction of the Federal Building on Eighth Avenue in 1939-40. Courtesy of Anthony Dimond Collection, Archives, University of Alaska, Fairbanks

After the outbreak of World War II in September 1939, rumors soon were rampant that the federal government planned to construct a military base in the Anchorage area. Actually, Alaska's delegate to Congress, Anthony J. Dimond, had asked Congress for military airfields and planes, army garrisons, and a highway link to the territory from the lower forty-eight states as early as 1933, but Congress did not appropriate any funds until 1940. In that year it made available monies for the construction of navy and army bases and a fort at locations ranging from Unalaska to Kodiak, and from Anchorage to Sitka. The building of these facilities, however, was to be stretched in a leisurely fashion over several years.

Anchorage citizens greeted the first contingent of troops on June 27, 1940. Engineers under the command of Major B. B. Talley began construction of the military base, first named Fort Richardson in honor of Brigadier General Wilds P. Richardson, the first president of the Board of Road Commissioners for Alaska from 1905 to 1917. The airfield was named Elmendorf to honor Captain Hugh M. Elmendorf, who had been killed in an aircraft accident at Wright Field in Ohio in 1933. Later, it became an air force base and retained the name Elmendorf while the army built its own fort seven miles distant toward the foothills of the Chugach Mountains and retained the name Fort Richardson.

In July 1940 Brigadier General Simon Bolivar Buckner arrived in Alaska to take charge of all military operations in the territory. Personally popular, he did much to establish friendly relations between the military and the civilian populations. However, serious housing shortages developed, and rents escalated. Soon scores of one and two room shacks appeared on the outskirts of the city, and builders developed raw, new subdivisions.

Military construction turned Anchorage into a boom town. This was reflected in population figures. On April 1, 1940, just before construction of the fort began, Anchorage had an estimated population of 4,000. A year later this had risen to 6,000, and by mid-summer 1941 to 9,000. This peak was maintained until December 1941. After the Japanese attack on Pearl Harbor the population dropped off because army families were evacuated. By April 1942 the population had stabilized at 6,000, which included all the military personnel and construction workers who were connected with the base but lived in town. Except for a few officers, all men in uniform lived at the fort outside of town and were not included in the total. Of the 6,000 living in Anchorage, it was estimated that 3,200 were men, 1,500 women, and 1,300 children under the age of eighteen. About seventy-five of the total were Alaskan Natives.

Irene E. Ryan recalls those eventful times. She first came to Alaska in 1932 for a year's stay, working as a waitress and bank clerk. She left and attended the New Mexico Institute of Mining and Technology where she earned a degree in geological engineering. After marriage

The interior of the Federal Jail in the '30s. The conditions in the jail were primitive. The pot-bellied stove provided the only heat. Courtesy of Anthony Dimond Collection, Archives, University of Alaska, Fairbanks

to John E. Ryan in 1938, the couple moved to Anchorage in 1941, at a time when the town's population began to explode because of the job opportunities offered by military construction. On arrival, they faced a severe housing shortage, so John built a 12 by 14 shack on rented land, with the only window in the door. They scrounged a stove from the dump and installed it on blocks in their shack. Mrs. Ryan started as a secretary for the Civil Aeronautics Administration and soon moved into an engineering position. They then bought a large and drafty two-story log house on Spenard Road, a considerable distance from town, but eventually sold the house and moved into civilian quarters on Fort Richardson.

Mrs. Ryan remembers that after the outbreak of the war a blackout went into effect. Cars drove with parking lights only, and on the base all windows were painted black with only a small slit in the center for daylight. In the face of a shortage of black paint, residents improvised and dissolved phonograph records in acetone and used the result as a paint substitute. As a precaution against possible Japanese air attacks, trenches had been dug. So whenever the sirens sounded, citizens were to vacate their homes and seek shelter in these trenches.

It was a tumultuous period, and as early as 1942, the City Council, in the hope of coping with the situation, had prepared a five year public works program with the assistance of the National Resources Planning Board. This plan called for extensive public works, including the

construction of a new airport, the improvement and extension of the water and sewage systems, health center, expansion of the telephone system, a community center and a high school and gymnasium, and general street improvements, among others. Some of these projects had gotten under way during the war, but most had to wait for the postwar period.

When the American forces drove the Japanese off Attu in May 1943 and landed on Kiska in August, they found that the enemy had departed under the cover of fog. Alaska no longer was a combat zone. Therefore, with the Aleutians secured, military activities declined sharply. From 152,000 members of the armed forces in Alaska in 1943, the number declined to 60,000 in 1945 and to 19,000 in 1946. Yet Anchorage optimists predicted the boom would continue because there were so many unmet needs, the most pressing of these totally inadequate housing. And there were hopeful signs, and one of these was the movement of several federal agency headquarters to Anchorage from southeastern Alaska. The Civil Aeronautics Administration, for example, built 100 housing units for its employees. Since Anchorage had tripled its population in five years, this growth placed severe strains on city services, and demands arose for a city manager form of government. When World War II ended in 1945, Anchorage had high hopes for the future.

The development of tensions between the United States and the Soviet Union after the war and the Cold War which resulted rescued Alaska

The Federal Building, constructed in 1939–40, replaced the old post office, the marshal's office, and the territorial jail on the "Federal Reserve" on Fourth Avenue. In addition to giving a boost to the economy, the building symbolized a commitment both to Anchorage and to the territory. Courtesy of Lulu Fairbanks Collection, Archives, University of Alaska, Fairbanks

from economic depression and obscurity. The territory's geographical position astride the northern Great Circle Route gave it a strategic importance in the free world, and once again brought thousands of troops and the expenditure of millions of dollars. Soldiers and construction workers who had been in Alaska during the war decided to return north and make Alaska their home, a fact reflected in population statistics: between 1940 and 1950, the territory's civilian population increased from approximately 74,000 to 112,000. During the same period, Anchorage grew from 4,229 to 11,254.

The Cold War forced American strategic rethinking: in the late 1940s, military planners decided on the so-called "heartland" concept of Alaska defense. This included virtual abandonment of the Aleutian Islands and proposals for massive military bases near Anchorage and Fairbanks. The new concept coincided with a general realignment in the overall strategic emphasis from the Pacific to the Atlantic.

But before the shift could be accomplished, massive problems had to be overcome in Alaska. Despite the frantic building activities during the war, the territory still had an inadequate system of communication and transportation, lacked housing, and had no modern economic and social infrastructure to support the defense

effort. Additionally, the territory's difficult terrain and weather conditions were permanent features to be reckoned with. The Alaska Railroad had to be upgraded, the Alaska Highway and the small road network needed improvements, and more housing had to be built. The military realized that vast expenditures were needed to provide basic facilities.

By June 1950, it had become apparent that some $250 million worth of construction would be undertaken. All was not rosy, however, because carpenters, electricians, and other craft unions had struck for higher wages. These work stoppages completely halted many projects and considerably slowed others. Workers, undeterred, had been flocking to Alaska from the States since early spring. Hoping for quick employment at high wages, they had slim resources and many suffered hardships because of the prolonged strike.

Eventually, however, defense spending made prices soar. Rentals were practically nonexistent in Anchorage, but workers earned big paychecks. Building mechanics, for example, received weekly paychecks which often exceeded $200 in addition to free board and room in remote locations. The basic daily wage of a waitress amounted to $8.60; that of a cook to $18.00. Members of craft unions such as

This 1940s aerial view shows at top center the wartime housing built at the end of the Park Strip between L and P streets. Courtesy of Anchorage Historical and Fine Arts Museum

plumbers and steamfitters, electricians, carpenters, and painters all made over $3.00 per hour. But prices corresponded with wages: fruits and vegetables, airborne, were exorbitant. Alaskan fresh milk cost 40¢ a quart; airborne from Seattle 54¢–55¢ a quart. Restaurant meals were high, a plain omelette or a lettuce or tomato salad came to $1.50–$1.75, and a piece of toast cost 30¢–35¢. Despite the prices, business boomed. Haircuts cost as much as $2.00, and blended whiskey $3.50–$4.00 a fifth.

While contractors hurried to complete military buildings, the influx of jobseekers continued, severely taxing Anchorage's housing and social services. City police reported a half-dozen murders in the first half of 1950 and blamed an increase in robberies on the boom conditions. Gambling flourished, and officials overlooked the illegal games so long as they were carried out in an orderly fashion. Municipal taxes from these activities may have influenced official leniency. Prostitution abounded despite the closing some years earlier of the red light district. The women now operated cautiously.

Despite many problems, Anchorage ultimately stood to profit from the turmoil of the boom. As a result of military construction, the private building sector thrived: the Government Hill Apartments for 696 families were built at a

cost of $10 million and the Brady-Smalling Construction Company built two 132 family housing units at a cost of $3 million. Many individual contractors built large and small modern houses with the help of Federal Housing Authority guarantees, and numerous subdivisions were developed. The city's suburb of Spenard counted 3,000 residents, and a modern shopping center was constructed on a tract which had been a part of Alaska's wilderness only five years earlier. The planned new airport rapidly took shape, and the professional and business communities expanded services.

A fifty-three-day walkout of the Sailor's Union of the Pacific in the summer of 1952 temporarily slowed the boom; yet, projects planned and underway continued.

Despite the fact that much needed yet to be accomplished, Anchorage, for the first time, offered bright opportunities for young professionals in addition to the customary seasonal employment for floating labor. The town, like the territory at large, was in a period of transition from which fewer and fewer people fled as soon as the weather turned cold each fall or a fortune had been made.

Still, Alaska's economy remained a largely seasonal one, dependent on the extraction of natural resources, such as fish, timber, and

The interior of the Hoyt Motor Company in the 1940s. Orville Jordet, a partner in the firm, is behind the counter. Courtesy of Norma Hoyt Collection

The Hoyt Motor Company was located for twenty-six years on the site of the present J. C. Penney building. In 1941 the staff gathered with their decorated truck. Courtesy of Norma Hoyt Collection

During a shipping strike in 1947 many Anchorage merchants brought supplies and equipment up over the newly opened Alcan Highway. Hoyt Motors drove up seven trucks and a car loaded with tires and other supplies. All the vehicles traveling to Alaska were held up at the Canadian border while shipping and customs problems were worked out. Courtesy of Norma Hoyt Collection

minerals. Transportation and tourism also played an important role. Then, on July 23, 1957, Richfield Oil Corporation drilled into the oil sands of what became the Swanson River field on the Kenai Peninsula, establishing Alaska's first truly commercial oil production. It was Richfield's first wildcat well in the territory, and the company had been lucky indeed, because the drilling rig, situated on the Swanson River oil structure, nearly missed the reservoir. Richfield completed its Swanson River Unit 1 on September 29, 1957, after drilling to a depth of 12,384 feet. Oil flowed from the discovery well at the rate of 900 barrels a day, also producing 122,000 cubic feet of gas. The company started a second well in the same year and completed it in 1958. Eventually, eleven other wells were drilled, thus outlining the boundaries of the Swanson River field.

The discovery did not result in a wild oil rush to the territory, but it did trigger a leasing boom in Alaska. By September 28, 1965, Alaska had held its fifteenth competitive lease since the first one, recorded on December 10, 1959. During those six years Alaska offered a total of 3,728,456 acres for lease, of which 66.9 percent, or 2,494,714 acres were snapped up by the oil companies. The lease sales had brought in $66,134,155, or an average of $26.51 for every acre leased.

Alaska was well on its way to becoming an important producer of hydrocarbons, and in October 1964, oil companies started to tap the oil resources of Cook Inlet when the stocky legs of platform A, the first inlet platform, were sunk into Cook Inlet's muddy bottom. Soon, the offshore platforms with their bright yellow gas flames flaring from the end of long booms became a common sight.

The oil discoveries added much to the economic stability of Anchorage, but other changes had occurred as well. By 1958 Alaska's road system had doubled, from a pre-war mileage of 2,400 miles of dirt and gravel roads.

The Alaska Highway and the Haines Cut-off had become all-year links.

The pre-war Alaska Railroad hauled freight and passengers along a single track 470 miles long from Seward to Fairbanks. Its equipment consisted of coal-burning locomotives and primitive wood-frame cars, handed down from the Panama Canal construction project. But by 1958, the Alaska Railroad right-of-way had been considerably upgraded, the rolling stock completely modernized, and the coal-burning locomotives replaced by diesel engines.

Most important, however, were the people who came to Alaska during and after the war, the majority of them members of a mid-twentieth century American urban industrial society, who expected and demanded the same standards of community living and services available in the lower forty-eight States. In addition, the expansion and change in the composition of Alaska's population in the post-war period resulted in increasing political agitation for self-government and the eventual attainment of statehood in June 1958 when the Senate passed the Alaska statehood bill. Within minutes after the news of the Senate's action was flashed north, air raid sirens wailed across Alaska, signaling not only the beginning of the territory's biggest celebration since V-J Day but also the end of differences of opinion among Alaskans about the merits of statehood. Typical was Norman Brown, the editor of the *Anchorage Daily News* and a harsh critic of the whole statehood movement. He wrote: "There is obviously but one thing to do. Everyone must now become members of the first team, pulling with every iota of his strength to make the state a success—to demonstrate to doubters everywhere that we are capable of running our own affairs from now on." Finally, President Dwight D. Eisenhower's signature on the official proclamation on January 3, 1959, formally admitted Alaska as the forty-ninth state to the union.

The 714th Transportation Corps, Railway Operating Battalion came to the aid of the Alaska Railroad in 1943. Because of the pressure of military freight, scarce labor, and deteriorating lines and equipment, help was needed to keep the railroad functioning under the demands of World War II. This unit was on duty until May 1, 1945. Courtesy of Anchorage Historical and Fine Arts Museum

Anchorage supported an active United Service Organization during World War II. The cache gave an authentic Alaskan look to the log building. This photo was probably taken in 1946. Courtesy of Anchorage Historical and Fine Arts Museum

The Anchorage City Band on the lawn in front of the City Hall. The City Hall building has been restored, as closely as possible, to its original appearance for use by the Alaska Pacific Bank and civic organizations. Courtesy of Lulu Fairbanks Collection, Archives, University of Alaska, Fairbanks

Anchorage was a military town during the 1940s. Citizens saw many jeeps on the streets and the sign "The Canteen" on Fourth Avenue. Courtesy of Machetanz Collection, Archives, University of Alaska, Fairbanks

CAPT. HUGH ELMENDORF
US AIR CORPS

In December of 1940, the War Department designated the new military field Elmendorf Field. Elmendorf Air Force Base was formally separated from Fort Richardson in 1950. Captain Hugh Elmendorf, for whom the field was named, was a pioneer in high altitude pursuit aircraft. He died while testing a new plane in 1933. Courtesy of Office of History, Alaska Air Command, USAF Photo

In early July 1940, Elmendorf Field was a tent camp. This view is across what is now Juniper Street near the intersection of P Street. The 4th Infantry camped on what was once the Arthur Marsh homestead. Courtesy of Office of History, Alaskan Air Command, USAF Photo

An Army inspection party in 1941. Lieutenant General John L. DeWitt is at the center, and Brigadier General Simon Bolivar Buckner, Jr. stands to the right with a portfolio. Courtesy of Office of History, Alaskan Air Command, USAF Photo

The ammunition area, Fort Richardson, in 1941. During the early years of establishing the military base, some facilities resembled scenes from the old west rather than a modern base in the mid-twentieth century. Courtesy of Office of History, Alaskan Air Command, USAF Photo

The Alaska Territorial Guard was organized during World War II to help protect the remote areas of Alaska as well as assist the general war effort. This painting by C. "Rusty" Heurlin was used as a recruiting poster and later to promote savings bonds. Courtesy of University of Alaska Museum

The Kashim Club was the first service club at Elmendorf Field, built at the instigation and direction of Marvin R. "Muktuk" Marston who was well known for organizing the Eskimo Scouts for the Territorial Guard. The building is now the Teen Center. Courtesy of Office of History, Alaskan Air Command, USAF Photo

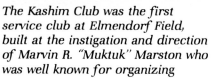

The elaborate building at Fourth and E at one time housed Hewitt's Drug Store. Across Fourth Avenue were the studios of KFQD, the oldest radio station in Alaska and the ninety-fifth to become licensed in the United States. KFQD went on the air in May 1924; in 1945 it was transmitting at 1,000 watts and serving Anchorage and the Matanuska Valley area. Courtesy of Anchorage Historical and Fine Arts Museum

FOURTH AVENUE
ANCHORAGE, ALASKA

Providence Hospital opened in 1939, run by the Sisters of Charity. They took over the care of the private patients who had been using the Alaska Railroad Hospital. In 1944 the old Railroad Hospital was turned into a dormitory and all patients were cared for at Providence Hospital, located between L and M streets and Eighth and Ninth avenues. Courtesy of Anchorage Historical and Fine Arts Museum

Fourth Avenue and C Street, shown about 1947–48, was one of the busiest corners in early Anchorage. The Lane Hotel followed the old Crescent Hotel. Courtesy of Anchorage Fur Rendezvous

The Loussac-Sogn Building is a modern block of stores and offices at the northeast corner of Fifth Avenue and D Street. Courtesy of Lulu Fairbanks Collection, Archives, University of Alaska, Fairbanks

Baseball continued to be a popular community activity. The Moose Baseball Team posed on a warm sunny day. Courtesy of Mary Dyer Collection

A fur sale at the Anchorage Fur Rendezvous in the early 1940s. The sale has remained one of the popular features of the wintertime festival for many years. Courtesy of Anchorage Fur Rendezvous

The Women of the Moose at a party at Mary Morrison's. Among those present were Mrs. McDaniel, Mrs. Spaulding, Mrs. Lickwold, Katleen Schoots, Dazy Heavens, Clara McCutcheon, Theresa Irwin, Bertha Nygadd, Edith Napp, Florence Green, Mary Morrison, Mrs. Matchi, Mrs. Ames, Mrs. Erickson, Lucy McDaniel, and Helen Matchi. Courtesy of Mary Dyer Collection

This group was called the Railroad-Anchorage Regular Volunteer Fire Department. Courtesy of Mary Dyer Collection

Many small airlines began in Anchorage and eventually merged to become some of the major lines we know today. Art Woodley founded Woodley Airways, which had a hangar at Merrill Field. The first Stinson A Trimotor stands in front of the company hangar. Woodley Airways operated between Anchorage and Juneau via Cordova and Yakutat as well as to points on the Kenai and westward to Bristol Bay. Woodley's firm evolved into Pacific Northern Airlines which in turn merged into Western Airlines in 1967. Courtesy of Anchorage Historical and Fine Arts Museum

Al Jones Airways, 1946, Merrill Field. Courtesy of Alaska Transportation Museum, Alaska Historical Library

Bob Reeve and his son Dick at Merrill Field in 1942. Two of the Reeve Airways planes are behind them, a Boeing 80A and a Fairchild 71. Courtesy of Richard Reeve Collection

After the war Anchorage began growing again. Here, at the groundbreaking ceremonies for the Government Hill housing area, are, left to right: Z. J. Loussac, Harry Lewis, unidentified, Leo Seidenverg, and Kenneth W. Kadow. Major General Stanley Scott and Colonel J. P. Johnson of the Alaska Railroad are using the shovels. Courtesy of Anchorage Historical and Fine Arts Museum

Colonel Johnson has been promoted to a tractor while Harry Lewis mans the truck. Perhaps this represented groundbreaking in a modern manner. Courtesy of Anchorage Historical and Fine Arts Museum

These intrepid skiers are at Arctic Valley, a popular local skiing area. Courtesy of Kay Kennedy Collection, Archives, University of Alaska, Fairbanks

A return to normal after World War II included Fourth of July parades and colorful floats. This scene shows the 1949 parade as it passed in front of the old Federal Building. Courtesy of Anchorage Historical and Fine Arts Museum

By the 1950s, Anchorage had begun to spread itself across the level land between the mountains and the sea. The Park Strip in the center of the photo had once been the southern boundary of the town. Courtesy of Kay Kennedy Collection, Archives, University of Alaska, Fairbanks

Fourth Avenue continued to be the center of business activity for many years. By 1945 streetlights and paving were in, but parking meters had not yet appeared. The Wendler Building is at the lower right at I Street. The sign on it advertises "Cambridge—Rooms." On the opposite corner is a gas station built in the mid-1920s and run by Oscar S. Gill, who was mayor from 1934 to 1935. Courtesy of Lulu Fairbanks Collection, Archives, University of Alaska, Fairbanks

The Fourth Avenue Theatre opened in 1947. It claimed itself the most modern theatre on the west coast with its lavish interior and extensive murals. Construction of the building was delayed by World War II. It probably benefited, however, by the continued planning of Cap Lathrop since it was, in many ways, the jewel of his commercial empire. Courtesy of Lulu Fairbanks Collection, Archives, University of Alaska, Fairbanks

The McKinley Apartment Building, now known as the McKay Building, was built in 1951. It was among the first "skyscrapers" in town and offered magnificent views from its windows. Courtesy of Machetanz Collection, Archives, University of Alaska, Fairbanks

In 1953, Zachary Loussac, mayor, signed an agreement for the purchase of $300,000 of City of Anchorage Library Bonds. Standing, left to right, are John Hellenthal, City Attorney; Ben Backe, City Clerk; and Bill Williams of Allison-Williams Company, Minneapolis. Seated at Loussac's left is George W. Marshall of Seattle, who purchased the issue with Williams. The others are city council members. Loussac, an early resident of Anchorage, established a foundation which continues to benefit the city he loved. The public libary is named for him. Courtesy of Anchorage Historical and Fine Arts Museum

In 1949 the Northern Commercial Company was one of the major department stores in Anchorage and a commercial success throughout Alaska. Their building on Fourth Avenue was located next to the Empress Theatre. Courtesy of Anchorage Historical and Fine Arts Museum

Denali School was brand new in 1950 when the proud teachers and students gathered outside for this photo. The Chugach Mountains are in the background. Courtesy of Norma Hoyt Collection

In March 1951 the Denali School PTA held a Jamboree to raise funds for playground equipment. Clowns and balloons were featured. Courtesy of Norma Hoyt Collection

The Alaskan Air Command Headquarters building was completed in 1948. It was named the Colonel Everett S. Davis Building in 1977 for the first commanding officer of Elmendorf Field and organizer of the Alaskan Air Force that preceded the Alaskan Air Command. The building is a handsome art deco structure and is significant today for its role as a command center. Courtesy of Office of History, Alaskan Air Command, USAF Photo

Alaska Railroad personnel posed in front of the engine that has been designated Alaska Railroad Number One and is exhibited at the Alaska Railroad Terminal Building. Colonel John P. Johnson was General Manager from 1945 to 1953. Left to right in the 1953 photo are, first row: George Sanderson, Bill Akers, Steve Harris, R. E. W. Simpson, E. J. Kunz, Charles Griffith, Col. J. P. Johnson, Bert Wennerstrom, John Triber, Ed Combs, F. W. Shelhorn, Tobe McClendon, Jesse Wallace, M. J. MacDonald, and J. J. Delaney. Second row: Carl Hahn, Newell Renner, George Benedict, Murray Hughes, Harold Brue, J. T. Flanagin, Richard Bruce, John Oberg, Olin Colip, Elroy Hinman, Bill Patterson, Paul Shelmerdine, Reino Vanajo, Harry Jones, Jack Karterman, John Manley, Speed Swift, Carl Meeks, I. P. Cook, C. O. Brown, Bruce Cannon, Anton Anderson, and Z. Tessendorf. Courtesy of Anchorage Historical and Fine Arts Museum

Bob Reeve posed in a snowstorm outside his Reeve Aleutian Airways office at 420 D Street in 1957. Courtesy of Richard Reeve Collection

Anchorage is one of the busiest air centers in the world. This scene from the 1950s shows an aircraft crossing sign on the road to the International Airport, where hangars and service facilities developed on both sides. Courtesy of Kay Kennedy Collection, Archives, University of Alaska, Fairbanks

The terminal building at Anchorage International Airport in 1953. The frame tower on the right had been brought from Yakutat for use until the tower in the center of the picture was completed. It was then moved to Lake Hood. After the new tower was destroyed in the 1964 earthquake, the old control tower was pressed into use again for the International Airport. It was finally dismantled in the late 1970s. Courtesy of Alaska State Department of Transportation and Public Facilities

Workmen are pouring the concrete floor in the FAA hangar under construction at the Anchorage International Airport on July 25, 1951. The hangar was in use until it burned in the mid 1970s. Photo by Hermann N. Kurriger; courtesy of Alaska State Department of Transportation and Public Facilities

Sea Airmotive, which became a major air charter service, operated out of these buildings in the mid-1940s. Lake Hood became a center for float plane operation after it was joined to Lake Spenard by a canal in 1938. Courtesy of James J. Rhode

At International Airport in 1957, Bob Reeve, former bush pilot and airline developer, is shown leaving a Douglas DC 4 used on the Reeve Aleutian Airlines Aleutian runs. Courtesy of Richard Reeve Collection

By 1916 the original townsite had been thoroughly cleared. Residents had landscaped their property and planted trees. These frost-covered birches decorated L Street before it was widened during the summer of 1959. Courtesy of Anchorage Historical and Fine Arts Museum

In 1954, the Stamp Club held an exhibition and reception. Courtesy of Anchorage Historical and Fine Arts Museum

July 4, 1959. This parade was special, however, because now their flag had forty-nine stars. Alaska had been formally admitted to state-hood on January 3, 1959. Courtesy of Anchorage Historical and Fine Arts Museum

Chapter Seven

After Statehood:

1960-1980

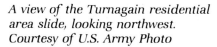

In 1950 the waterfront continued to be an active area with canneries, docks, small boats, and railroad traffic. Courtesy of Anchorage Historical and Fine Arts Museum

A view of the Turnagain residential area slide, looking northwest. Courtesy of U.S. Army Photo

Although Anchorage continued to grow slowly, the first years of statehood were financially difficult ones. Then, on Friday, March 27, 1964, one of the greatest recorded earthquakes of all time, measuring from 8.4 to 8.7 on the Richter scale, struck southcentral Alaska and in a few minutes caused extensive damage. Fortunately, the loss of life was relatively low, but property damage was estimated at approximately $380 million at a minimum and almost $500 million at a maximum. Although Anchorage was very hard hit, its citizens almost immediately began the task of reconstruction. Technicians and mechanics arrived to restore essential services while medical teams and rescue units fanned out through the 900-mile coastal arc, which had been ripped by more than ten million

times the force of an atomic bomb, to minister to the injured and to prevent typhoid epidemics. Space was made available for the 2,000 homeless in Anchorage alone. Most of the office buildings in the center of Anchorage were destroyed or severely damaged, and one store sank so far into a fissure that only its roof showed on the buckled street level. Industry and the federal government responded swiftly and effectively hence southcentral Alaska recovered and rebuilt quickly.

Population statistics reflected the continuous growth. Anchorage boasted of a population of 44,237 in 1960, up from 11,254 in 1950, while the total population of the state had increased in the same period from 128,643 to 226,167. By 1979, the municipality of Anchorage,

with an area of approximately 1,884 square miles, contained an estimated population of 184,775.

Perhaps more important to the area's growth, Anchorage International Airport had become one of the busiest in the nation. As early as 1954, the Civil Aeronautics Administration had announced that Anchorage was the fourth busiest center in the nation in air traffic operations—overshadowing such metropolitan centers as San Francisco, Houston, Miami, Denver, Dallas, Cleveland, and Honolulu. These figures applied only to civil aviation, excluding military activities on the nearby bases. A look at the geography of Anchorage shows why it became important in the air age: it is located at the top of the world where today's jet air routes

between Europe and Asia, and between North America and those two continents, come together. Anchorage can therefore claim to be the "Crossroads of the Air World," a fact which has made it a stopping point for numerous intercontinental airlines.

As the 1970s began, Anchorage found that it also occupies the strategic spot in its own state. It is the midway control point and headquarters for the Alaska Railroad, operating between the ports of Seward and Whittier and between the interior Alaska railhead and roadhead of Fairbanks. It also sits at the hub of a web of paved roads and highways which links it directly to the oil and industrial centers of the Kenai Peninsula, to the North Slope oil fields, and to the Alaska Highway, which provides a road connection

Tillie Reeve drove the Pioneer King and Queen Regents in the 1960 Fur Rendezvous Parade. Sitting next to her is Admiral Jim Russell. The old Presbyterian Church at Fifth Avenue and E Street is in the background. Courtesy of Richard Reeve Collection

through Canada to the other states. Anchorage has not only become the financial, service, and oil capital of Alaska but also it has developed its own port facilities, in the process becoming the busiest seaport in the entire state.

Anchorage's great population changes had come in the 1940s and 1950s with the construction, and later expansion, of the state's two largest military bases in the immediate Anchorage area. The two bases, Elmendorf Air Force Base, which houses the unified Alaskan Command, and the Army's Fort Richardson were built just north and east of the city. Today they employ thousands and continue to make a large, stable contribution to the economy.

Oil and gas production on the Kenai Peninsula and the offshore waters of Cook Inlet, as well as the subsequent spin-off of a modest petrochemical industry, provide another prop to the economy. And although Fairbanks was

the prime beneficiary of the new Prudhoe Bay oil discoveries on the North Slope, Anchorage nevertheless became the headquarters city for the oil companies involved.

By 1979 Anchorage's position as the state's financial, service, and transportation center was undisputed. The greater Anchorage area also contained almost half of the entire state's population. Statistics show that almost half of all available jobs in the Anchorage area are in the distributive industries. More than a third are in federal, state, and local government, and about 15 percent in what are considered the basic resource extractive industries. Anchorage is also the headquarters for nearly two-thirds of the jobs in Alaska's construction and trade service industries and about half of all of the federal jobs in the state.

Along with growth and opportunities, problems have developed as well. Anchorage

Bob Reeve at the Reeve Aleutian Airways office displays some of his famous collection of photographs and memorabilia about 1960. Courtesy of Richard Reeve Collection

has become a sprawling city, with traffic jams, lack of recreational and community facilities, and inadequate downtown parking.

This concentration and diversity of employment assures Anchorage's continued growth and prosperity. But in addition, the city also offers all of the amenities of modern, urban American life, while at the same time giving its residents abundant opportunities and easy access to outdoor recreation. The city has two daily papers, the morning *Anchorage Daily News* and the afternoon *Anchorage Daily Times.* The only statewide Native paper, the *Tundra Times,* is also published here. Anchorage also boasts of six radio and four television broadcasting stations. Over 100 churches represent a wide spectrum of denominations. Most nationally affiliated adult and youth groups are represented by at least one branch or chapter in the Anchorage area, in addition to many social,

school, and special interest groups as well. Over the years Anchorage also has developed excellent medical facilities with numerous hospitals, about 365 physicians, surgeons and other specialists engaged in private practice or employed by the municipality, state, or federal governments. More than 70 dentists practice as well.

Cultural opportunities abound. There are two universities and one community college, and the Z. J. Loussac Public Library, located downtown, has seven branches in the area. Music, art, and drama flourish. The Symphony Orchestra, Community Concert Association, various music clubs, Civic Ballet, Little Theatre, Alaska Repertory Theatre, and collegiate groups all offer concerts and productions. The Anchorage Historical and Fine Arts Museum and several art galleries offer varying exhibits.

Anchorage also has parks and playgrounds,

161

swimming pools, community and recreation centers, and a municipal golf course. Earthquake Park, containing 135 acres, is located at Knik Arm at the west end of Northern Lights Boulevard. The mounds of earth thrown up like high ocean waves are a constant reminder to the citizens of the gigantic forces unleashed on Good Friday in 1964 which devastated so much of southcentral Alaska.

To the north the Matanuska and Susitna valleys offer abundant opportunities for outdoor recreation, as does the Kenai Peninsula to the south where residents go hunting, fishing, clam digging, canoeing and boating, and hiking. Only forty miles to the south is Alyeska Ski Resort, with snow the year round in the upper reaches, and there are skiing opportunities closer to the city itself.

In a very short time, the city on the shores of Cook Inlet has developed from its beginnings as a tent town on the flats of Ship Creek in 1915 to the sophisticated metropolis of Alaska in the 1980s.

On July 8, 1961, the Port of Anchorage was dedicated; Harold Strandberg, Chairman of the Port Commission and Jane Bodich, Miss Port of Anchorage, posed at the commemorative plaque. The port facility, which has steadily grown, was designed to improve conditions for shipping and to make Anchorage a major port. Courtesy of Port of Anchorage

Anchorage has become a major stop for flights between Europe, Asia, and the United States. The international flight ramp already showed a great deal of activity in the late 1960s. Courtesy of Alaska State Department of Transportation and Public Facilities

Float planes tie up all along the shores of Lake Hood and Lake Spenard. The little buildings along the shore are used for storage. Courtesy of Alaska State Department of Transportation and Public Facilities

The Alaska National Guard moved in to help the stricken community. The north side of Fourth Avenue between C and D was lost to the slide. Courtesy of Anchorage Earthquake Collection, Archives, University of Alaska, Fairbanks

The earthquake of March 27, 1964, affected many parts of Anchorage, but the familiar stretch of Fourth Avenue from B to E streets was almost completely destroyed. The intersection of Fourth and C is in the foreground. Courtesy of U.S. Army Photo

This was the north side of Fourth Avenue looking west. Courtesy of U.S. Army Photo

J. C. Penney's store had just recently opened before the earthquake. This scene is near the corner of Fifth Avenue and D Street. Courtesy of U.S. Army Photo

The post-earthquake scene at Fourth Avenue and D Street looking east shows the venerable Lane Hotel at the right. The sign advertises a production of Our Town *at Alaska Methodist University. Courtesy of U.S. Army Photo*

This photo was taken at 5:48 p.m. during the quake on March 27, 1964. The U.S. Army Band and National Guard officers were *knocked down by the quake. Courtesy of Anchorage Earthquake Collection, Archives, University of Alaska, Fairbanks*

An Alaska National Guardsman sleeps between shifts on security guard duty in the Turnagain area, March 30, 1964. Courtesy of *Anchorage Earthquake Collection, Archives, University of Alaska, Fairbanks*

The spirit of the people of Anchorage is perhaps exemplified by this sign painted on a house in the Turnagain area to let searchers know that the family survived. Courtesy of Anchorage Earthquake Collection, Archives, University of Alaska, Fairbanks

Rebuilding after the earthquake included the laying of water and sewer lines to devastated areas and to new areas being developed. Courtesy of Anchorage Historical and Fine Arts Museum

The Anchorage Westward Hotel dominates this 1965 view across the earthquake-devastated area on the north side of Fourth Avenue. The hotel is the successor to the Anchorage Hotel and is located in the same area along Third Avenue. Courtesy of Anchorage Historical and Fine Arts Museum

The Anchorage Fur Rendezvous, popularly known as Rondy, is a major winter festival. Based on older community gatherings and dog races, the Rondy was formally organized in the mid-1930s. The World Championship Sled Dog Race carries on the old tradition. Parades were always important, too, and in 1979 the Susitna Valley High School Band marched past the old Federal Building on the right. Courtesy of Anchorage Fur Rendezvous

By 1965, the city was beginning to fill its large level plateau and was beginning to grow upward as tall buildings appeared on the skyline.

Recovery from the earthquake was rapid. The railroad runs below the bluff where Third Avenue curves into L Street at the lower left.

Resolution Park is now located at that point. Courtesy of U.S. Army Photo

The Fur Rendezvous takes advantage of the benefits of winter. Here, on an improvised ice rink in front of the old Federal Building, curlers demonstrate the game to an attentive audience. Courtesy of Kay Kennedy Collection, Archives, University of Alaska, Fairbanks

A National Forest float for the 1968 Fur Rendezvous parade promoted various kinds of winter sports activity in the Chugach National Forest. The forest provides an open area for the growing population. Courtesy of U.S.D.A., Forest Service, Chugach National Forest

This Eskimo blanket toss was a popular attraction during the Fur Rendezvous. In recent years many Yupik Eskimos from southwestern Alaska have visited Anchorage, and some have settled here as well. Anchorage has a large Native Service Hospital, and many Natives use this facility. In addition, a number of Native regional corporations have their offices in Anchorage. Courtesy of Tourism Collection, Alaska Historical Library

The Fur Rendezvous is a community event. A troop of Cub Scouts assisted in putting together the premium book in 1979. Courtesy of Anchorage Fur Rendezvous

The Rondy parade includes participants from many civic organizations, such as the Anchorage Jaycees in 1979. Photo by Pete Robinson; courtesy of Anchorage Fur Rendezvous

Alyeska, near Girdwood, was becoming a major ski resort by March 1966. The base of one of the chairlifts has attracted a crowd. The day lodge is at the left. The resort uses some land that is within the Chugach National Forest. Courtesy of U.S.D.A., Forest Service, Chugach National Forest

The Anchorage Historical and Fine Arts Museum groundbreaking in 1967 was the beginning of one of Alaska's important museums, providing a broad range of cultural services to the community. Included in the ceremony were Mary Louise Rasmuson, Herb Hilcher, Evangeline Atwood, Bill Creighton, Norma Hoyt, Wilda Hudson, Richard Silberer, and Elmer E. Rasmuson. Support for the new museum came from the Cook Inlet Historical Society and the local arts community. Courtesy of Anchorage Historical and Fine Arts Museum

The Anchorage Symphony has been a source of pride for the community for many years. Maurice Dubonnet was the conductor during the 1979–80 concert season. Ruth Jefford was the concertmaster.

Here they are shown at the Performing Arts Center at the Anchorage Community College. Courtesy of Anchorage Symphony Association

The Operalaska program is educational in purpose and among its activities provides in-school performances of opera for assemblies and classes. In 1980 they performed Christopher Columbus by Offenbach. Kelly Kerr and Rick Krzeczkowski are singing, Claire Wipperman is at the right, and Susan Wingrove is at the piano. Courtesy of Anchorage Civic Opera Association

The Anchorage Civic Opera Association production of the Mikado in March 1979 had a dramatic set and elaborate costumes. Michael More, in the center of the stage, played the lead roll of Nanki-Poo. Courtesy of Anchorage Civic Opera Association

Anchorage has been an All-America City twice, first in 1956 when it was the first city so designated outside the contiguous United States. The second award came in 1965 in recognition of the effort made by the community after the 1964 earthquake. Sister city programs were carried out with Chitose, Hokkaido, Japan, and Tromso, Norway. Whitby, Yorkshire, England, became a sister city in recognition of Captain James Cook's association with that city. This sign was in front of the City Hall on Fourth Avenue during the Christmas season in 1980. Rowinski Photo

The Anchorage Community College campus on Providence Drive was under construction in the 1970s.

Anchorage Community College, established in 1952, is the largest of the community colleges serving the state as part of the University of Alaska. Post-secondary students may study in their field of interest from vocational subjects to liberal arts. Courtesy of Anchorage Community College

The Anchorage Community College is a pleasant setting for studying or for sitting out of doors on a warm summer afternoon. Courtesy of Anchorage Community College

A historic meeting between President Richard Nixon and Emperor Hirohito of Japan took place on Elmendorf Air Force Base in September, 1971. Hirohito was the first ruling member in the 2,500-year history of the Imperial dynasty ever to set foot on foreign soil. The Empress and Mrs. Nixon are on the platform with them. Courtesy of Office of History, Alaskan Air Command, USAF Photo

Alaska Methodist University, founded in 1957 to provide private post-secondary education in Alaska, opened to students in 1960. It has an attractive campus in the Goose Lake area. In 1978 the name was changed to Alaska Pacific University to reflect the new scope of the school's interests. The Campus Center, at left, was designed by Edward Durell Stone, the internationally known architect. Courtesy of Alaska Pacific University

The University of Alaska, Anchorage, has a developing campus that presents a wide range of college courses and serves the major population center of the state. It is located southwest of downtown Anchorage in an area that also includes the Anchorage Community College and Alaska Pacific University campuses. The new Providence Hospital is also close by. Goose Lake is part of a citywide park system and is a popular swimming area. Chester Creek Park is a wooded area that extends into the city, above and to the left of the lake. Courtesy of University of Alaska, Anchorage

The Wendler Building stands today surrounded by the Captain Cook Hotel. Although it has been remodeled, it retains the character of a "townsite" building. The Club 25 is a restaurant, owned and run by the daughter of A. J. Wendler, Mrs. Myrtle (Wendler) Stalnaker. Courtesy of Anchorage Convention and Visitors Bureau

The Consortium Library at the University of Alaska, Anchorage, was built in 1972. It was designed in cooperation with Alaska Methodist University and located so it could serve both schools. Courtesy of University of Alaska, Anchorage

The Pioneer School was built in 1915 by the Alaska Engineering Commission to meet the needs of the children in the new town. Although it was considered inadequate, it was used as a school until December 1916, when the new school was completed. The building was also used by the Pioneers of Alaska for many years at a new location at Sixth Avenue and E Street. After the 1964 earthquake, it was moved to its present location at Third Avenue and Eagle Street, where it still serves the community as a meeting place. Rowinski Photo

Kimball's Dry Goods is still in business in the Kimball Building at Fifth and E, which was built in 1915. In spite of all the changes around it, the building and the shops retain much of the flavor of old Anchorage. Courtesy of Anchorage Convention and Visitors Bureau

Dr. Roland Lombard is a regular contestant and frequent winner in the "Rondy" races. He and his team are coming down Fourth Avenue with the McKay Building in the background. Courtesy of Anchorage Fur Rendezvous

The Anchorage Historical and Fine Arts Museum at Seventh Avenue and A Street, which is supported by the city, offers exhibits of Native Alaskan cultural materials as well as changing art exhibitions and many special programs. Courtesy of Anchorage Historical and Fine Arts Museum

The 1980 Fur Rendezvous featured dog races as usual on Fourth Avenue. Although the dog team is reminiscent of older scenes when Fourth Avenue was really a part of the trail system, the setting has changed considerably: even the snow must often be brought in for the races on the cleared streets. Courtesy of Anchorage Fur Rendezvous

The view across the Ship Creek Basin today shows a busy industrial area with the cranes of the Port of Anchorage at the base of Government Hill. Rowinski Photo

The road to the Ship Creek Basin, down C Street and across to Government Hill, has been replaced by an overpass that provides access to Elmendorf Air Force Base, the Port of Anchorage, and the busy industrial area. Rowinski Photo

The new control tower for the
International Airport was completed
in the late 1970s. It also serves the
Lake Hood float plane operation.
Courtesy of Alaska State Department
of Transportation and Public
Facilities

Japanese tourists have increased in
Alaska as Anchorage has become a
stop for many foreign airlines. A
visitor in traditional costume views
Portage Glacier, which is easily
accessible from the city. Courtesy
of U.S.D.A., Forest Service, Chugach
National Forest

BUILDING IT UP

The forest began thousan...
not as tree seeds, because they could not...
on the sterile site....

but as spores of hardy kinds of plants called LICHENS. Lichens are adapted by their very specialized nature to live on bare rock

WHEN DEFORMING FORCES IN THE EARTH'S CRUST EXCEED THE PLIABILITY OF THE ROCK, A RUPTURE CALLED A FAULT RESULTS. AN EARTHQUAKE IS CAUSED BY THE SHOCK OF FRACTURE AND THE SUDDEN DISPLACEMENT OF THE EARTH'S CRUST.

EARTHQUAKE

WE MIGHT THINK OF THE *Lichen* AS BEING PRIMITIVE OR SIMPLE, BUT SEE HOW MARVELOUSLY DESIGNED IT IS.

PORTAGE RIVER BRIDGE

Earthquakes are comm... building. Almost 1000... 120 of which may... Good Friday ear... more land area... square miles or m...

ing - the land is ac...ally
Building - uplif...
...dden.

PORTAGE VA...
ACTIVE ZONE
THE EVIDENC...
IS CLEAR.

SPLAY-
EN

history,
cubic miles
...hin the mountain,
...arby valley, filled
...ne the "Valley of 10,00...

...CK, HAS OFTEN BEE...
...KY. THE ICE OF PORTA...
...ST, CARRIES IN IT A REC...
RECORD IS BEING USED...
GEOLOGIC P...

A naturalist at the Visitor Center at the Portage Glacier explains the geology of the area to young visitors. Courtesy of U.S.D.A., Forest Service, Chugach National Forest

As part of their environmental education program the Forest Service sent a trailer equipped with staff, programs, and exhibits to local schools. These students at Campbell School are examining a beaver in March 1970. Courtesy of U.S.D.A., Forest Service, Chugach National Forest

Avalanches in the Alyeska Winter Sports area can pose a hazard to skiers. The upper gun mount is used to control snow buildup in the popular skiing area. Hill manager Don Conrad and Snow Ranger C. O'Leary examine the terrain in February 1968. Courtesy of U.S.D.A., Forest Service, Chugach National Forest

The Chugach National Forest, which once included the Anchorage bowl, is still easily accessible. It stretches from the Kenai Peninsula to the Copper River Delta and includes mountains, glaciers, seacoasts, and major rivers. The campgrounds are popular weekend and vacation destinations. Courtesy of U.S.D.A., Forest Service, Chugach National Forest

The late Senator E. L. (Bob) Bartlett spoke at the dedication of Andy Simons Mountain in the Chugach National Forest in July, 1967. Ben Benson, who designed Alaska's flag in a childhood competition, is at the right. Simons was the first licensed hunting guide in Alaska and spent much of his life on the Kenai Peninsula. Courtesy of U.S.D.A., Forest Service, Chugach National Forest

A new Federal Building on Seventh Avenue brings together many of the agencies that serve Alaska. The new building replaced the Federal Building of 1939 on Fourth Avenue. Rowinski Photo

The Visitor Information Center at Fourth and F streets, an old style log cabin with sod roof, was built in 1954 by the Junior Chamber of Commerce. It is a good starting place for visitors to Anchorage who want information on the attractions and facilities available in Anchorage today. Courtesy of Anchorage Convention and Visitors Bureau

A borough-wide bus system uses this new terminal on Sixth Avenue. Rowinski Photo

Fifth Avenue has become a major business street with a trend toward taller buildings. The glass structure at Fifth and I is called the Fifth Avenue Building. Rowinski Photo

The Loussac Library, at Fifth Avenue and F Street, honors Zachariah Loussac, who arrived in the tent city after living in many gold camps including Iditarod. His first drugstore in a tent grew into many successful businesses and Loussac's social and civic involvement included three terms as mayor, 1948-50. Rowinski Photo

The Forest Service Avalanche Patrol on a mountain overlooking Cook Inlet. The highway at the base of the mountain, along the edge of Turnagain Arm, is made safer by careful observation of the snow pack and weather conditions. Courtesy of U.S.D.A., Forest Service, Chugach National Forest

The Pioneers Home in Anchorage on Eleventh Street provides housing and care for senior residents. The modern building is already acquiring a new addition. Rowinski Photo

Workers on one of the platforms in Cook Inlet drill a new well. Courtesy of University of Alaska Museum location. Courtesy of University of Alaska Museum

Captain James Cook looks out over Cook Inlet from Resolution Park, which commemorates his exploration of Cook Inlet in 1778. Rowinski Photo

Bibliography

Atwood, Evangeline. *Anchorage: All-American City*. Portland, Oregon: Binfords & Mort, 1957

Barry, Mary J. *A History of Mining on the Kenai Peninsula*. Anchorage, Alaska: Alaska Northwest Publishing Company, 1973.

Beaglehole, J. C. *The Life of Captain James Cook*. Stanford California: Stanford University Press, 1974.

Carberry, Michael E. *Patterns of the Past: An Inventory of Anchorage's Heritage Resources*. Municipality of Anchorage: Northern Printing, 1979.

Mongin, Alfred. *An Evaluation of Anchorage Cultural Historic District: A Proposal to Determine Eligibility for the National Register of Historic Places*. Anchorage, Alaska: Alaska Division of Parks, 1976.

Naske, Claus-M., and Slotnick, Herman E. *Alaska: A History of the 49th State*. Grand Rapids, Michigan: Wm. B. Eerdmans Publishing Company, 1979.

Sherwood, Morgan, editor. *The Cook Inlet Collection: Two Hundred Years of Selected Alaskan History*. Anchorage, Alaska: Alaska Northwest Publishing Company, 1974.

Wilson, William H. *Railroad in the Clouds: The Alaska Railroad in the Age of Steam, 1914– 1945*. Boulder, Colorado: Pruett Publishing Company, 1977.

Magazines

Alaska Industry, May 1970; May 1972; May 1973; May 1975; May 1976; May 1977; May 1978; July 1979; July 1980.

Unpublished Works

Department of the Interior. Alaska Engineering Commission. Report of the Manager. Land and Industrial Department, April 12, 1916 to September 30, 1916. Record Group 126. National Archives.

Department of the Interior. Alaskan Engineering Commission. Report of the Manager. Land and Industrial Department, October 1, 1916 to December 31, 1917. Record Group 126. National Archives.

Naske, Claus-M. *Alaska's Four Proposed State Parks*. Anchorage, Alaska: The Alaskan Environmental Group, 1972.

Oral History of Pioneer Women of Alaska. Interviews with Irene E. Ryan, November 6 and 10, Anchorage; Lorene Harrison, August 26, 1980, Anchorage; Doris Walkowski, August 22, 1980, Anchorage.

Index

A

Aberdeen Cannery   25
Admiral Watson   52
Alaska Engineering
    Commission   49, 53, 78-79, 81
Alaska Labor Union   68, 90
Alaska Methodist University   182
All Saints Episcopal Church   111
Anchorage Air Transports   10
Anchorage Civic Opera
    Association   179
Anchorage Community
    College   181
Anchorage Fur Rendezvous   139,
    171, 174-76, 186
Anchorage High School   116-117
Anchorage Historical and Fine Arts
    Museum   178, 186
Anchorage Public School   71-72
Anchorage Symphony   178
Annie W.   53
Arnold, Lt. Col. Henry   120
Arctic Fishing Co.   24
Aviation   103, 113-114, 119, 141,
    151-153, 159, 163

B

Bank of Alaska   90
Barndollar, B. H.   75
Bartlett, Sen. E. L.   195
Beresford, William   18
Brown, Jack   36, 113

C

Cape Elizabeth   17
Cape Saint Hermogenes   17
Chamber of Commerce   90
Christensen, Andrew   56, 59
Christian Science Church   58
Chugach National Forest   36-37,
    192, 195
City Hall   75, 180
Clark, Ora Dee   71
Coleman, Ike   92
Congregational Church   58, 96
Cook Inlet Pioneer   36, 62-64
Cook, Captain James   17-18, 203
Corea   22
Crow Pass Trail   27
Curten, Joe   46

D

David, Anna   95
David, Leopold   35
Delaney, J. J.   114
Denali School   149
DeWitt, Lt. Gen. John L.   135
Dixon, George   17

E

Earthquake   159, 165-70
Elmendorf Field   134, 136
Empress Theater   93

F

Federal Building   128, 195

Federal Court House   126
Federal Jail   127

G

Gerig, William   75
Gore, John   17
Government Hill   46, 83, 129, 142

H

Hansen, F.   75
Harding, President Warren G.   102,
    108
Hoover, President Herbert   109
Hope   31
Hotel Anchorage   64
Hoyt Motor Co.   130

I

Islander   82

J

Jackaloffi, Evan   21
James, Mrs. Casy   65

K

Kenai Cannery   25
King, Lt. James   17
Knik   30-36

L

Lathrop, Capt. Austin E.   122
Laurence, Sydney   115

Lawrence 77
Lombard, Dr. Roland 185
Loussac Library 199
Loussac, Zachary 148

M
Maps 16, 18, 40
Marmot Island 17
Mason, C. L. 75
Masonic Temple 70, 110
Matanuska Colony 106-07,
   121, 123
McCutchen, Mrs. Fred 98
McDonald, Zsmerelda 94
Meares, John 17
Mears, Frederick 41, 43, 75
Merrill, Russell 10, 114
Mount St. Augustine 17

N
Nixon, President Richard M. 181
Northern Commercial
   Company 148

O
Odale, John L. 30
Ohlson, Col. Otto F. 116

P
Pacific Grocery Company
   Wholesale 75
Palmer, G. W. 36

Parsons, Mrs. Jessie 98
Pioneers Home 200
Podboy, Ernest 89
Pollar, George E. 108
Portage Glacier 36
Portage Pass 18
Portlock, Nathaniel 17
Potter Creek 82
Presbyterian Church 58, 110
Providence Hospital 138

Q

R
Red Cross 86
Riggs, Thomas 76
Roman Catholic Church 58
Ryan, Irene E. 126

S
Saint Hermogenes Isle 17
Ship Creek 37, 41, 42, 44, 47,
   103-05
Shonbeck, Art 10
Snug Harbor 26
Spenard, Joe 69
S. S. Alameda 106
Steese, James G. 109
Stetter, Herman 31
Strandberg, Harold 162
Strong, John F. 42
Sundberg, Mrs. Peter 98

Sunrise 30

T
Tanaina Indians 17
Tyonic 25, 37

U
University of Alaska 182-83

V
Van Campen, Helen 43
Visitor Information Center 196

W
Warren, H. P. 75
Wetherbee, H. M. 23, 26
Whitworth 102
World War I 62
World War II 126-27, 132-36

Y
YMCA 80